Postmodern Revisionings of the Political

Thinking Gender
Edited by Linda Nicholson

Also published in the series

Feminism/Postmodernism
Linda Nicholson

Gender Trouble
Judith Butler

Words of Power
Andrea Nye

Femininity and Domination
Sandra Lee Bartky

Disciplining Foucault
Jana Sawicki

Beyond Accommodation
Drucilla Cornell

Embattled Eros
Steven Seidman

Erotic Welfare
Linda Singer

Materialist Feminism and the Politics of Discourse
Rosemary Hennessy

An Ethic of Care
Mary Jeanne Larrabee

Feminist Epistemologies
Linda Alcoff and Elizabeth Potter

Gender Politics and Post-Communism
Nanette Funk and Magda Mueller

Engenderings
Naomi Scheman

Feminist Theory and the Classics
Nancy Rabinowitz and Amy Richlin

Postmodern
Revisionings
of the Political

ANNA YEATMAN

ROUTLEDGE   NEW YORK   LONDON

Published in 1994 by

Routledge
29 West 35th Street
New York, NY 10001

Published in Great Britain by

Routledge
11 New Fetter Lane
London EC4P 4EE

Library of Congress Cataloging-in-Publication Data

Yeatman, Anna.
    Postmodern revisionings of the political / by Anna Yeatman.
       p. cm.
    Includes bibliographical references and index.
    ISBN 0-415-90197-9. -- ISBN 0-415-90198-7 (pbk.)
       1. Critical theory. 2. Postmodernism. 3. Feminist theory.
    I. Title.
    HM24.Y42 1993
    301'.01--dc20   93-33597
                                                   CIP

British Library Cataloging-in-Publication Data also available.

Contents

Preface   vii

Introduction: Postmodern Critical Theorizing   1

I THE POLITICS OF REPRESENTATION
AND INTELLECTUAL AUTHORITY

1 The Epistemological Politics of
   Postmodern Feminist Theorizing   13

2 Postmodern Epistemological
   Politics and Social Science   27

3 The Place of Women's Studies in
   the Contemporary University   42

II REFIGURING THE POLITY

4 Beyond Natural Right: The
   Conditions for Universal Citizenship   57

5 Minorities and the Politics
   of Difference   80

6 State and Community   92

7 Postmodernity and Revisioning
   the Political   106

   Notes   123

   Consolidated Bibliography   130

   Index   137

Preface

This is a book of essays written largely over the period of 1990–1992, which is to be taken as a contribution to postmodern critical theory. The principal thread of argument running through these essays is the proposition that we cannot and should not evade the postmodern moment, a moment which poses important challenges for emancipatory social movements and their understanding of the business of politics. Indeed, I suggest that the emancipatory movements of the postcolonial era are postmodern in character.

It can be conceded that the task of working reason and difference (universalism and relativity) together is one both difficult and subject to unresolved debate, without thereby rejecting the task itself, and the postmodern moment it connotes. As Schrift (1990, 110) proposes, "We can perhaps locate an aporia at the very center of postmodern thinking: the problem of devising legitimating criteria for even the provisional exercising of authority." This is a problem tackled at various points in these essays, and I signal clearly my own belief that such criteria can be devised even though they are without transcendent authority. (For extended and useful debate about this issue see the essays in Benjamin, 1992.) If there is a postmodern political project, it lies here. This being the case, it bears emphasis that it is *post*modernism rather than *anti*modernism that informs my politics. As Burbules and Rice (1991, 397) suggest, "The 'post' implies a moving beyond, of course, but also a continuity; any tradition identifying itself as post-something is also accepting the basic significance of the tradition it proposes to go beyond."

There are present here two other primary and, it turns out, interconnected lines of argument. The first of these entails the proposition that a postmodern emancipatory politics does not abandon the values of modern universalism and rationalism, but enters into a deconstructive relationship to them. This is an important point to grasp, since so many have taken postmodernism *tout court* to entail such an abandonment. Then they have turned around—not inappropriately, given their assumption—and achieved the not-too-difficult feat of showing that postmodernism depends on the very premises it attributes to the discourses of modernity. Turner (1990, 6) exemplifies this kind of criticism of postmodernism:

> ...the prospects of creating a "genuine" postmodern social theory are...diffi-cult for reasons that Habermas has potently outlined. He argues, for example, that Foucault is caught in the paradox of the "performative contradiction", because Foucault is ultimately forced to use the tools of reason which he wants to overthrow. In short, can anti-foundationalism exist without founda-tions?

It is specious to suggest that Foucault wants to overthrow the tools of reason. This is not the line of fracture between postmodern and modern(ist) thought. Instead it concerns the authority and the nature of reason. Where moderns turn their enquiry on the question of the conditions of right reason, postmoderns interrogate the discursive economies of the different versions of right reason that we have inherited. Postmoderns insist on the exclusions which these differ-ent economies effect. They desacralize reason, they do not reject it. Specifically they attempt to work reason and difference together.

It is arguable that Hegel, one of the great modern philosophers, works with difference. His narrative in the *Phenomenology* of the education of mind is one where the development of mind works through what might be taken to be crises of identity, where at each point the crisis arises from what the identity of mind is forced to marginalize or to leave out. Hegel, however, commits himself to the premise that these crises are subsumed within a progressively more adequate, inclusive and self-identical rational consciousness which reaches the ultimate telos of absolute truth. As postmoderns—at least those who identify with con-temporary emancipatory movements—endlessly reiterate, this is a construction of reason which authorizes as it legitimizes a single and exclusive standard bearer of truth. This subject is authorized to represent all who preceded it in time as immature and undeveloped, and all who are othered by its self-identical properties as equally immature and undeveloped.

The third line of argument insists on the normative-political project which resides in the postmodern, deconstructive relationship to the modern values of rationalism and universalism and to the kind of democratic order they have informed. This is true at least of those postmoderns whose critical stance is informed by their shared positioning as the other of modern reason. This posi-tioning carries over into the structures of modern citizenship: those who are positioned as other to reason find themselves also marginalized in relation to cit-izenship status and rights. For example, the reiterated exclusion from full citizenship status and rights of women, non-English-speaking-background Australians, people with disabilities and Aboriginals is evident in their discur-sive placement within the category of "special needs groups" in Australian public policy of the 1980s (see Yeatman, 1990b, especially chapters 5, 7 and 8).

Those who have been othered by the categories of modern citizenship have been placed in a peculiar relationship to the institutions of modern democracy. On the one hand, they demonstrate the partiality of these institutions, the abrogation of their professed adherence to universalistic standards of right, by exemplifying how these institutions systemically exclude considerable numbers and various categories of people. On the other hand, the very conduct of this demonstration is in the name of these universalistic standards.

Critics of postmodernism take this contradiction to be further grist to their mill. They assume that it is obvious that it does not make sense to be contradictory in this way. A postmodern emancipatory politics insists that it does make sense. This is precisely the point they are arguing, namely that universalism is never achieved: all particular universalistic institutions establish boundaries for their being which operate a particular economy of inclusions and exclusions. They cannot be corrected; all that can be done is to substitute a new order of inclusions and exclusions. This is not necessarily immaterial: it may mean a substantive step in respect of correcting particular wrongs. Political contestation of the exclusions or inequalities which follow from a particular order of governance is in the name of a universal. Within the space that opens up for contestation, debate and dialogue between the established order of governance and a contestatory movement, a universally oriented politics does develop (see Rancière, 1992; and my use of his argument in Yeatman, 1993).

In these essays, then, the postmodern moment is interpreted from a political point of view. By entering into a deconstructive relationship to the modern emancipatory project, this postmodern politics can be seen to transform this project and, in this sense, to pursue it. If universalism does not reside in what is, or even in what could be, but lies instead in a political, contestatory space that opens up in relation to existing wrongs and to those who contest them in the name of equality, it is clear that this has radical implications for the nature of political vision. Postmodern emancipatory vision does not offer a utopian future, but works to develop contestatory political and public spaces, which open up in relation to existing systems of governance.

To speak to the eight essays collected here, there is considerable coherence of concerns across them. In general, they broach the question of the nature and standing of postmodern politics in its relationship to modern rationalist emancipatory politics. Postmodern politics is associated with the contestation of what are taken to be core assumptions or values within modern democratic/emancipatory politics, namely:

- the construction of the bases of political community with reference to an order of being that is placed both prior to and outside politics because it is accorded a given ontological status (this order of being may be the liberal "natural" individual or what is taken to be a naturally or customarily grounded citizen community);

- a univocal construction of reason, and thus the idea of rational consensus as the regulative ideal of conflict and debate within the democratic polity;

- a construction of the subject of politics as subsumable within an uncontested universal and impartial sovereign subject (Locke's political authority, Rousseau's General Will, Hegel's and Marx's universal historical subject);

- a construction of rationally grounded knowledge as objectively based in the sense of lying outside or beyond the contestability of what is taken to be subjective opinion.

The hallmark of a postmodern emancipatory politics is taken to be its insistence that meaning, truth, identity, right and community are all values that lie *within* a politics of representation. Thus these values do not precede representation—as classical theorists of representation would have it—but are constituted within the domain of representational praxis. They are thoroughly contestable concepts, and the distinguishing mark of postmodern politics concerns the acceptance and working of this point.

Postmodern emancipatory politics is thoroughly dependent on the ontological investments of modern politics. These investments are those that concern the value of individual self-determination and its relationship to the self-determining properties of the citizen community or polity. The kind of emancipatory politics of difference which critical postmodern/feminist theorizing pursues is weakly developed unless it understands its dependency on the values of modern universalism, rationalism, justice and individualism. If this is the case, then postmodern emancipatory politics is located in a deconstructive relationship to modern emancipatory politics. It is the nature of this relationship which many of these essays attempt to explore and to specify.

Among other things, this requires examination of the way in which a postmodern, decentered, open and legitimate politics of voice and representation recasts the role of the sovereign state. In modern democratic theory, reconciliation between individualized political will and the sovereign authority is effected by subsuming the former as a particular under the latter's universality. This produces a number of well-known problems (discussed here primarily in Chapter Five). All democratic visions of the polity as an arena of contest and debate presuppose a regulative, sovereign normative authority. Here it is argued (after Lyotard) that the postmodern sovereign authority is recast in terms of the formal and cybernetic value of performativity, which is perpetually challenged by, even while it is dependent upon, those who assume in relation to this authority the identity of its contestatory others (see Chapter Eight).

There are more specific themes which recur in different parts of the book:

- the politicization of knowledge in the context of a politics of difference where rational enquiry is reshaped in terms of an open epistemological politics of voice and representation;

- a defense of the values of professionalized knowledge, and of the university as the site of rational inquiry, as critical supports for civic and democratic process, and as able to offer an important critical and reflective aspect to the contemporary politics of identity;

- an interest in the epistemological positioning of subaltern intellectuals and their different and conflicting lines of intellectual and political accountability, a difference which indicates their positioning across audiences;

- the conditions for a democratization of professional authority, one where the value of professional expertise is not surrendered but relocated in a partnership relation to the expressed needs of the professional's clients.

It remains to be said that these essays have been conceived over a period during which I changed countries, from Australia to New Zealand. An Australian, I lived in Adelaide and worked at the Flinders University of South Australia for many years. In April, 1991, I took up appointment as the Foundation Professor of Women's Studies at the University of Waikato in Hamilton, New Zealand. As I write this preface, I am aware of my planned return to Australia in June, 1993, to take up a chair of Sociology at Macquarie University in Sydney.

New Zealand and Australia are two white-settler societies in which the colonizers have come from British stock. In this these societies are alike. In many other respects they are very different. One such difference concerns the way a postcolonial politics of difference is constituted in the two. In New Zealand, this politics is oriented in terms of a bicultural dialogue between its indigenous people, Maori, and those whom Maori call *Pakeha*, the white settlers whose ethnic origins link them into the history of British colonization and settlement of New Zealand. In Australia, a postcolonial politics of difference uneasily yokes together multiculturalism (a recognition that a third of contemporary Australians are of non-English-speaking background), and a much less developed rhetoric of both redressing white-settler wrongs committed against Aboriginal Australians and of respecting Aboriginal aspirations for self-determination. In each of these two societies there is a vigorous women's movement. Like their counterparts elsewhere, the New Zealand and Australian women's movements have been culturally oriented and organized in terms of the dominant ethnic—in this case, the white settler—voice. At the same time, it is arguable that white-settler feminism is a symptom of white-settler postcolonial aspirations for independence from the mother metropole. This is a poorly understood mediation of these feminisms, as is their interpellation as movements which are required to respond to the contemporary postcolonial politics of difference in these two societies. While these essays foreground postmodernism rather than postcolonialism, they are to be read against this backdrop of preoccupations.

Acknowledgments are due especially to Moira Gatens, Joan Landes, Paul Patton, Di Gursansky, Philippa Rothfield, Vicki Kirby, Barry Hindess, David Levine and Andrew Sharp for conversations or for access to their work in ways which have helped to shape these essays. Special thanks are due to both Linda Nicholson and Maureen MacGrogan for their encouragement and patience, and to Neill Bogan for his careful and intelligent editing. In getting this work to press, I am acutely aware of the students—both graduate and undergraduate—who, especially at Flinders University, but also at the University of Waikato, supported this project by their interest in and engagement with the issues at a time of considerable resistance to postmodernism in the academy. I think especially of Heidi Nietz, Stefan Ridgeway, Sandra Dalton, Valerie Hazel, Sue Duncan, Robin Peace, Robyn Longhurst and Petra Oerke.

An earlier version of Chapter One first appeared as "Postmodern Critical Theorisings: Introduction" in a special issue of *Social Analysis* (no. 30, 1991), on "Postmodern Critical Theorising." Chapter Two is the revised version of a piece which first appeared in *Social Semiotics*, volume one, number one, 1991. Chapter Three is a slightly different version of a chapter by the same title in Kathleen Lennon and Margaret Whitford, eds., *Objectivity, the Knowing Subject and Difference: Essays in Feminist Epistemology*, London: Routledge 1993. Chapter Four is a revised version of my Inaugural Lecture at the University of Waikato, which has appeared in a slightly different form in *Women's Studies Journal* (New Zealand), volume 8, number 1, 1992. Chapter Five first appeared in *Social Concept*, volume 4, number 1, 1988. Chapter Six is the revised version of a piece which first appeared in *Political Theory Newsletter*, volume 4, number 1, 1992. Chapter Seven was first presented in the University of Auckland 1992 Winter Lecture Series and in a different version will be a chapter in a book edited by Andrew Sharp forthcoming from Auckland University Press. Chapter Eight is the slightly revised version of an essay which first appeared in *Social Analysis*, number 30, 1991.

Anna Yeatman,
University of Waikato,
January 1993.

Introduction
Postmodern Critical Theorizing

Postmodern thematics, issues and approaches are now well developed within the terrain of social and political theory. While postmodern thought represents intellectual currents which cross over the established disciplines of modernist social science, and is sometimes consciously developed as a postdisciplinary endeavor, it is also making inroads into the intellectual agendas of these established disciplines. However, this is not a peaceful process. As anyone involved in this intellectual politics is aware, postmodern currents of thought arouse in many a passionate defense of modern(ist) intellectual paradigms. This is primarily because of a postmodern, perspectivalist approach to knowledge where the central anchor of the modern(ist) episteme—reason—is refused universal and transcendent status. Instead, postmodern thought develops a thoroughgoing epistemological politics, which insists on the always embodied and always particularized nature of reason. Reason is always tied to the pragmatics and the politics of the particularly contextualized nature of knowledge claims. The consequence of this for how reason actually operates is, as Lyotard (as interviewed by Riejen and Veerman, 1988, 278) put it: "There is no reason, only reasons."

What this means precisely is subject to debate. Some would take this to indicate that postmodernism realizes that fearful prognostication of Yeats, "the center will not hold," with ensuing *anomie* for social science. A perspectivalist theory of knowledge is seen to introduce a nihilistic pluralism within which there is no possibility of rationally arbitrating multiple and contested knowledge claims. From Plato's *The Republic,* Western civilization has associated the grounds of virtue and justice with reason, where reason represents access through knowledge to the grounds or truth of being. In this context, postmodernism threatens the integrity of this civilization, and seems to imply the abandonment of all that makes this civilization "civilized," namely skeptical of the authority of tradition, open to change, critical of unreflectively held values and knowledge, and democratic.

1

This is one reading of postmodernism which makes good sense from the standpoint of those oriented within the culture of the modern Enlightenment. The defense of modernity in these terms is becoming more sophisticated as it is placed in an interlocutory and antagonistic relationship to postmodern challenges. For example, Habermas's defense of an intersubjectivist paradigm of communicative action, where, ideally, epistemological politics is regulated by an unconstrained and rationally oriented consensus, is one which accepts the embeddedness of knowledge within the pragmatics of social action while it retains the idea of transcendent or universal standards of validity (see Habermas, 1987). In respect of this embedded quality of knowledge, there is much in common between Habermas and postmodern perspectivalist approaches: both reject the monadic sovereign rational subject of Cartesian philosophy, whose adherence to a transcendental reason is matched by his own "transcendence" of his social context. However, they part company in relation to the status of standards of validity. Habermas (1984) insists that such standards are those which unconstrained, rational consensus would derive in relation to the various distinct spheres of argumentation (theoretical discourse, practical discourse, aesthetic criticism, therapeutic critique, explicative discourse). Moreover, without such standards, there lacks a criterion for judging the adequacy of what presently exists by way of such argumentation (and the institutions which it informs), thus permitting a construction of truth or right, for example, which is independent of common sense, popular fads and powerful vested interests. Postmodern perspectivalism does not do without standards of validity, but insists that they cannot be accorded transcendent status. This is because postmodern perspectivalism withdraws legitimacy from the kind of rational consensus Habermas believes in principle to be possible. There being an irresolvably complex polyphony of voices and irresolvable difference between them, all that is possible is pragmatically oriented and provisional, negotiated agreements. Since a settlement is held to be a function of an historically specific communicative pragmatics, and to have the characteristics of negotiated and provisional agreement rather than rational consensus, the politics of any one particular settlement are legitimately open for acknowledgment, discussion and challenge. They do not have to be subsumed and thereby occluded within the ideal of rational consensus.

However, this raises the question of whether postmodern critical theory is prepared to accept just any negotiated settlement. Or to turn it around: whether certain transcendental norms are embedded within the very idea of negotiation? As proposed above, postmodern critical theory commits itself to certain standards of validity in respect of what conduces to an open, democratic politics of voice and representation. If this necessarily ties postmodern critical theory into a modern (Habermasian/neo-Kantian) insistence on transcendent criteria of right and justice, its relationship to this insistence is deconstructive in nature.

Postmodern critical theory has to accept that these criteria are transcendent in the sense of providing regulative norms for the very dialogic possibilities of contestation, debate and negotiation. However, by insisting these norms are creatures of discourse, it brings out their contestable nature. Let me explain. In meta-discursive terms the conditions of a negotiated settlement may be universal—for example, agreement not to further strategic objectives by assassination and other forms of coercion—but these conditions exist here only in the abstract. In respect of any particular, historical, negotiated settlement, conditions such as guarantees of freedom of expression for contestatory voices are themselves subject to contested interpretation, to irreducibly multiple perspectives. For example, in New Zealand at the present time, Maoris are likely to see due process in respect of a disputed claim as requiring that the rights and wrongs of the claim be heard on the relevant tribal *marae* or meeting place. *Marae* procedure and conceptions of due process are different from those of the Anglo/*Pakeha* legal system. How are these two proceduralist conceptions to be reconciled, and can they be? Especially bearing in mind that the one interpellates a tribal subject, the other an individualized subject? If they cannot, what are the kinds of adjudication and proceduralism required which respect this difference in ways that are adequate to the case at hand? This is a very real question preoccupying different sectors of the New Zealand system of governance (in its broad, Foucauldian sense). If postmodern critical theory does not provide an answer to this question at the present time, its virtue is that it is able to admit the question and begin to work with it.

Postmodern intellectual currents from the standpoint of adherents of modern intellectual traditions must appear rather different than they do from the standpoint of those of us who are attempting to work with, and out of, postmodern perspectives. We are clearly sympathetic to postmodernism. However, this does not mean that our relationship to postmodernism is uncritical. It must be clear that it is possible to accept that the postmodern condition is real, in the sense of something we have to contend with and cannot wish away, without taking this to mean that our relationship to this reality takes on the features of a positivistic acceptance of it.

Acceptance of the reality of the postmodern condition means a relinquishing of a nostalgic holding on to modern(ist) standards of reflection and critique. Of course, there are postmodern sympathizers who espouse a positivistic relationship to the postmodern condition. Theirs is a more or less ironically inflected, skeptical, playful, but fundamentally quietist relationship to postmodernism, to, for example: the informatics revolution and the ways in which information and its distribution have become central to the accumulation of capital and to the state-centered business of politics; the hyperreality of a consumption-oriented society, where the artifice of the copy is seen to improve on, to even perfect, the original; a society of silicon breast and penile implants, a society where what Haraway calls "cyborgs" become a natural way of imagining, thinking and seeing; a globalized social environment in which issues of redistribution increasingly assume a North/South conflictual character, where it becomes entirely reasonable to those identified with the North (the West, the First World) for *LA Law* to turn one of its cases on a Los Angeles public hospital selling an organ for kidney transplant to a "rich alien" rather than providing it as a matter of public service to an ordinary American citizen.

Postmodern positivism is exemplified in the US-led coalition's conduct of the Gulf War in early 1991 by: 1. the tactical emphasis on high-tech weapons, and the conversion of Middle East desert conditions into a hyperreal setting for a demonstration of Western technological superiority; 2. the priority placed on the management of representations of the rationale for, and conduct of, this war, through a tightly controlled deployment of the electronic and print media by the military command; 3. an almost celebratory and certainly unapologetic representation of the West as justifiably dominant in a Third World context. What is postmodern about this? Might has been right throughout the history of Western colonialism. This time, however, the assertion of Western imperial purpose and power is in relation to a developed and mature context of postcolonial movements and politics. If the US's successful prosecution of the Gulf War healed the wounds of national honor and pride in relation to US defeat at the hands of a national liberation movement in Vietnam, the Gulf War is a distinctly new type of imperial venture. It is one that is designed, not to civilize the natives, but to ensure that they are not allowed to implement the traditions of Western democracy in ways that take their own national societies out of the control of Western *imperium,* or worse, lead them to challenge their own increasing immiseration in the face of Western extraction of surplus from them by means chiefly of creditor/debtor relationships. If serendipity (and a good deal of Western military support and aid) produced Saddam Hussein as just the baddie required to remind us of how the West was won, the singular virtue of this venture was to occlude democratic struggles in the so-called Third World by rendering Hussein the metaphor for all Third World leadership and thereby erasing from historical memory leaders associated with struggles for national liberation and independent nationhood (Nasser, Nkrumah, Ho Chi Minh, Salvador Allende).

I am suggesting that there is a postmodern Western imperialism, one that openly espouses Western dominance in the face of sustained contestation of this dominance in *the name of democratic and civilized values.* This imperialism is conducted at home as abroad. At home Western-identified state societies have abandoned the rhetoric of social citizenship, a rhetoric that underpins one of the core discourses of the welfare state, and which was the fruit of intracultural struggles for citizenship on the part of the working class and women. These struggles were conducted and institutionalized in ways which presupposed cultural homogeneity, and a nationalism which conflated the boundaries of the citizen community with an agnatic kinship order. It is arguable that once those who fell outside this order—in Australia, for example, Aboriginals and (non-Anglo/Celt and non-English-speaking) "migrants"—began to construct legitimate claims on the discourse of social citizenship, in ways which necessarily required it to be recast, the process of its abandonment began.

Arguably, the difference between the emancipatory social movements of the 1960s, 1970s and 1980s, and those which had been oriented to the welfare state politics of an earlier era, is that the former were situated within a web of affiliations with postcolonial movements. These movements were themselves complex, entailing movements challenging internal colonialism from *within* Western state societies (e.g. the US Civil Rights movement), and from *without* on the part of newly independent states or of those struggling to become independent. There were important connections between these two types of postcolonial movements, between, for instance, the US Civil Rights movement and the Pan-Africanist, non-aligned politics of newly independent African states in the late 1950s and early 1960s. Western emancipatory rhetorics began to be shaped within a narrative of connections between class exploitation, Western colonial dominance, patriarchy and state-sponsored ethnic assimilationism. Inevitably, and necessarily, these rhetorics began to explore difference.

In so doing, these rhetorics have opened up a postmodern terrain of critical theorizing and emancipatory politics. They are postmodern, precisely because they could not totalize the differently motivated emancipatory struggles and convert them into the voice of the one, singular and rational subject. Theirs is an emancipatory politics of exploring what it means to develop the pragmatics of self-determination when there is no self in question, only selves who are positioned in different ways.

The abandonment of a singular, universal subject of humanity for whom the whole drama of modern emancipation was designed has had important consequences for emancipatory politics. If there is no singular, universal subject, then the business of emancipation itself has no self-evident warrant in a theory of what it means to be human (philosophical anthropology). Such theory turns out to be ethnically marked by the specific self-interpretation of the modern West (see Derrida,1982).

Even allowing for the necessity and the importance of philosophical-anthropological assumptions about what it is that human beings have in common, the construction of what they share must be always at a high level of generality. S.P. Mohanty (1989, 21), in an important article dealing with the issues raised by the abandonment of the humanist Subject, shows the politico-ethical value of "positing the following minimal commonality between us and them: the capacity to act purposefully, to be capable of agency and the basic rationality that the human agent must in principle possess." As seasoned veterans of the contestable terrain of philosophical anthropologies are too well aware, the minute these propositions are further specified their contestability becomes all too evident. Rational choice theorists interpret this minimal commonality in ways importantly different than neo-Kantians such as Weber (1968) who not only identified different *types* of rational action but did so in respect of the different kinds of meaning-constitutive activity they entail.

Emancipation may always have something to do with human beings understanding themselves to be in some kind of autonomous relationship to their capacity for agency. This is the common ground shared by democrats of all hues, rational choice theorists included. Mohanty is correct that the sharing of this common ground is the condition of respect for, and understanding of, struggles for emancipation different from those which are familiar to "us." He is also correct that to concentrate on the term of difference as such is to introduce a relativism and, ultimately, a diffidence in relation to a plurality of different struggles. Such a diffidence ensures that little or no effort is given to working on the larger vision which may take up the connections between, and even the commonalities of, these struggles.

These points notwithstanding, it remains the case that different emancipatory movements mobilize their own historically specific construction of that minimal commonality Mohanty identified. These constructions cannot be subsumed within the inevitably ethnocentric reinstatement of a universal Subject of human agency. They specify incommensurabilities as much as they rely on commonalities in respect of human agency. For example, feminist specifications of agency tend to be incommensurable with masculinist specifications of agency, a point that Chodorow (1978) took up in her contrast between the relational characteristics of women's individuality and the atomistic characteristics of men's.

A philosophical anthropology, then, cannot ground a shared narrative of emancipation. At the same time, emancipation loses any anchorage in a teleological account of humanity, whereby the progressive development of humanity is its journey into the light of reason and a society free from domination.

Postmodern emancipatory politics conducts itself without the certainties and direction provided by a rationalist utopianism. Its emancipatory orientation is strictly pragmatic, that is, oriented to the contemporary politics of movements which have adopted and reshaped the modern(ist) imaginary of self-determination. There is no more warrant for their being than their historical existence. It follows that what we can know about these movements has to be conducted in relation to how they enter the whole business of the politics of voice and representation. If we are to know something about them we need to listen to how they represent themselves. There is no Reason which permits us to know those movements to which we do not belong, independent of their own self-representations. This means that subjects, who are positioned outside the self-advocacy politics of a particular movement, cannot legitimately appropriate the representations of that movement for their own purposes. If there are to be legitimate connections made between differently positioned representations these have to arise out of negotiated agreements constructed by the differently positioned social actors coming together to work on the terms of their coexistence.

There being no Reason, in the singular, the utopian vision of reason bringing into being a society free from domination has lost all credibility. The utopian aspect of postmodern imaginaries of self-determination lies not in that kind of rationalist millenarianism, but in the visionary aspects of particular, everyday struggles for social change. These cannot be totalized into the one big, great struggle, and, thus, the idea of a revolution loses cogency. This does not preclude an emancipatory consciousness of seeking to build connections between the various struggles for self-determination, to explore their affinities, and to acknowledge their differences.

The metaphor of emancipation itself cannot be allowed to pass without some comment. In modern usage this metaphor connotes an act or action whereby individuals or a people are released (or release themselves) from some kind of bondage into freedom. Postmodern usage withdraws any sense of completion or finality from this idea of release. Emancipation is always relative to an established, discursive order which is already of the past, a new discursive order with its own peculiar modes of domination having been ushered in through the process of emancipation.

The acknowledgement of difference has brought about a loss of discursive innocence. The transparency of good intentions guarantees nothing, and the ideal of transparency is a dangerous illusion, encouraging as it does various forms of moral terrorism practiced on self and others. Instead, good intentions are always in service to a particular discursive regime, and a discursive regime is structured by its own unique discursive economy of distribution of inclusions and exclusions. This is a political consciousness which is decidedly anti-millenarian, and to the extent utopia is tied up with millenarianism, dystopian.

This being the case, it follows that the relationship of postmodernism(ity) to modernism(ity) is quite different in nature from the relationship of modern (r)evolutionary narratives to what they represent as pre- or non-modern types of society. In these narratives, modernity is opposed to the societal types which preceded it: modernity represents the dynamics and telos of enlightenment, the triumph of reason over unreason, of society over nature. The difference between modernity and pre(non)modernity is arraigned in terms of a developmental antinomy which confirms the status of modernity as representing the social norm. This is the kind of difference or otherness which is invoked in order to establish an identity of the same.

Marxist narratives of modernity divide modernity into two epochs: a capitalist epoch which develops the technical conditions for freedom from domination, a freedom which presupposes social mastery over nature; and a post-capitalist epoch which realizes this possibility of freedom from domination, and which is brought about by a conscious commitment on the part of the mass and agent of humanity (the proletariat) through a revolution. The conception of modernity as representing a clean break with what precedes modern society remains the same, and these narratives represent a variation on the general theme of an Enlightenment commitment to the idea of modernity as a rational society.

What is noteworthy about postmodernism(ity) is that this idea of a clean break is not operative. Postmodernism(ity), in fact, does not suggest that somehow society has moved on from modernity in the sense of becoming something other than modernity. The "post" in postmodernism(ity) indicates a relationship of continuity, even dependency. "Post" suggests that it is possible now to bound the project of modernity, to discern its features, to understand the kind of paradigm it comprises. This is possible only because there has developed a vantage point of skepticism and even critique in relation to this paradigm. Unlike modern critical theory and revolutionary politics, postmodern critical theory and oppositional politics call into question the fundamental premises of the project of modernity. These premises all hinge on the modern commitment to a rational project of societal progressive development which involves the progressive mastery of society over nature.

If there is such a vantage point of skepticism, it seems to logically follow that there must be some emergent new paradigm heralding a new epoch. However, for various reasons, it is not clear that this is the case. First, postmodernism questions the modern construction of historical time in terms of linear *progress*. It does not represent itself as a progressive development in relation to modernity. Rather, depending on which version of postmodernism is in view, postmodernism places itself in a critical interrogative and/or oppositional relationship to modernity. In terms of what might be regarded as normative periodization, postmodernism shares common ground with contemporary environmentalist movements. Since these movements question the pragmatics of the modern project of progressive technological mastery of nature, and require us to begin to enter a pragmatics of working within an ecological model of ourselves in relation to a complex and finite natural universe, they place themselves outside a linear model of time. They are neither regressive in respect of modernity—for they do not ask us to give up our rational, problem solving and technical capacities but to redirect them—nor progressive. It is a conception of time that belies both modern, and what moderns like to think of as traditional time. Traditional time works within circular conceptions of origins (birth), maturation, and decay (death). While environmentalist models of time respect life-cycle time where it makes sense to do so, this does not preclude the adoption of linear time models of learning through technical experimentation. Nor does it preclude a syncretic bringing together of these two models of time. Environmentalist time is more like the time of "art"—of reflective practice undertaken with a craft orientation—than that of science, but in it scientific progress is not eschewed: rather, it is placed in harness to the art of living with nature in an advanced technological age.

Note that this syncretic sense of time maintains a relationship to modernity even while it resituates and redefines the modern project. This point bears emphasis. Precisely because postmodernism works with the idea of knowledge as situated, it finds it entirely natural to accept that knowing subjects are positioned within the discursive traditions that have formed them. Postmoderns have to work with the traditions of modernity. Postmodern discourse is shaped in terms of this relationship. In this sense, there is a strong symbiosis between postmodernism and modernism. As I have suggested, the critical difference lies in the postmodern refusal to accept the founding myth of modernity: the development of society in accordance with a universal and transcendent reason. Yet, if postmodernism rejects this heroic form of reason, it works comfortably with reasons. Thereby, it is not placed outside rationalism, and, inevitably, it owes an enormous amount to the tradition of modern rationalism and its internal critiques.

It is worth reflecting further on why it is we have developed terms like postcolonialism and postmodernism. No one suggests that colonialism is no longer with us, at least none of the postcolonials do: indeed their point is precisely the opposite. Postcolonialism, however, is a term which suggests that the classic age of modern colonialism is over, and has given way to more subtle forms of colonialism which are adapted to the era of independent statehood. Postcolonialism, thus, connotes: 1. a time subsequent to that of classical Western projects of colonization; 2. an oppositional relationship to contemporary forms of Western colonialism which undermine and sabotage the self-determining aspirations of the citizenries of independent states; and, 3. a normative ideal of postcolonialism to guide these oppositional struggles.

Postmodernism is a more ambiguous term, lending itself as we have seen to both critical and positivistic relationships to a postmodern condition of the modern institutions of capitalism, the market and the state. When postmodernism assumes a positivistic connotation it is in recognition that these modern institutions have been qualitatively altered by the new age of informatics, globalization and the kind of postcolonial social complexity connoted by the new social movements of the 1960s, 1970s, 1980s. When postmodernism assumes critical connotations, it is a term which behaves very much like that of postcolonialism. Its brings together the following connotations: 1. a new time for the modern institutions of capitalism, the market and the state: they have entered a postmodern age, which gives them qualitatively distinct characteristics from their modern form (see Castells, 1989); 2. an oppositional relationship to the univocal and monocultural project of modern rational mastery, and to postmodern forms of reshaping this project so that it survives by domesticating the legitimation of cultural and social difference; 3. a normative ideal of postmodernism as authorizing the opening up of a democratic politics of voice and representation, where the ideal state is not the overcoming of domination once and for all but ongoing imaginative and creative forms of positive resistance to various types of domination.

I have offered here an alternative reading of postmodernism from that which associates it with a nihilistic relativism and anomie. Undoubtedly, there are such currents within postmodernism. However, there is an emancipatory postmodern politics which has a strong relationship of continuity with modern traditions of emancipatory discourse. This politics is reshaping and resituating emancipatory norms within a postmodern thematics. In respect of its intellectual expressions, it may be termed postmodern critical theorizing.

Part One

The Politics of Representation and Intellectual Authority

1

The Epistemological Politics of Postmodern Feminist Theorizing

Introduction

Over the course of the 1980s, feminist theorizing and postmodernism entered into a relationship which is transforming both of them. Feminist theorizing has introduced into postmodernism the politics of voice and representation. Very often the elaboration of this politics has been undertaken by postcolonial feminist theorists who have been compelled to take up these issues of voice and representation in respect of "western" feminism.

Not all feminist theorizing has entered into this sometimes ambivalent, sometimes exuberant and always creative relationship with postmodernism. However, even where feminist theorizing remains tied into the distinctly essentialist presuppositions of liberal, radical and socialist feminism, this theorizing cannot continue innocent of postmodern feminist theorizing and its embrace of the politics of difference. To the extent that this is true, and to the extent that postmodernism appears to be the discursive terrain on which the politics of difference is being currently played out, feminism and postmodernism can be understood as in a relationship of reciprocal interpellation.

The epistemological politics of postmodernism is its most determinate and perhaps most interesting feature. This is an epistemological politics which contests and forswears the foundationalist presuppositions of modern and modernist discursive formations. These are presuppositions which ground the validity of knowledge claims with reference to some *a priori* ground of truth, beauty and justice. This ground is a monocentric universal guaranteed by the unitary subject of mankind, god or nature. These are interchangeable terms in modern thought, as the idea of Reason bears out.

Postmodernism represents the thoroughgoing critique of what Ryan (1988, 559) terms "the classical theory of representation, which held that meaning or truth preceded and determined the representations that communicated it!" It pursues the Saussurean revolution which makes the meaning of representations a function of the system of significations to which they belong. Reality no longer precedes but becomes constituted by representations. In postmodern and poststructuralist approaches the Saussurean concept of a closed system is abandoned in favor of an historically contingent, determinate but not closed, discursive or representational formation.

The lack of closure follows from the dialogical, interdiscursive properties of how discourses belonging to this formation are cosituated (see Todorov on Bakhtin, 1984; and Threadgold, 1986). This cosituation becomes a relationship of historical imbrication, where even oppositional discourses are symbiotically entwined with dominant discourses. For example, postcolonial discourses are dialectically related to, and specified in terms of, contemporary imperial discourses of western, metropolitan dominance (e.g. the discourse of "restructuring"); and *vice versa.* At the same time dominant discourses by the terms of their exclusions and deferrals specify the discursive grounds on which a politics of contested absences develops. This is the point at which a politics of representation links up with a politics of difference.

In the politics of representation (see Shapiro, 1988; Ryan, 1988; John, 1989), representations become understood as political practices which distribute unequally power and other goods. The contestation of these practices, which constitutes a politics of representation, cannot proceed independent of complicity with these practices. There is no privileged position "outside" the semiosis of a particular representational formation. Contestation, thus, does not explore an autonomous, alternative representational space. Instead, it works with the contradictions, heteroglossia, and historically contingent features of a specific representational or discursive formation.

When a politics of representation comes together with a politics of difference, there develops an explicit and openly contested opposition between those representations which impose a monological, discursive order of performativity, technology and science and those which belong to subjects interpellated as the excluded other of the monological discursive order. When these subjects explore their voices as the excluded other they perforced investigate their discursive positionality as both an historically specified excluded other and as a complicit, if subordinate, subject interpellated within the discursive formation of monological dominance.

To be subsumed as a complicit subordinate within the master subject's "mankind" ("society," "nation," etc.) and as a subject excluded from being able to speak on behalf of—that is, "represent"—this unitary construct, constitutes a complex positionality. As long as the excluded other operates a politics of inclusion, it is a revisionist politics with respect to the monological universal and no more. The excluded other still does not have a voice. Her politics has not opened up the discursive space which makes this voice possible. Not surprisingly, a condition for this discursive space is the multiplication of excluded others contesting their distinctive types of exclusion: not just gender, but race, ethnicity, sexuality, disability and so on. The multiplication of the grounds of difference permits difference as such to emerge: it is not swallowed up in the monological politics of inversion which a binary political contest requires.

Difference poses a new set of requirements for how the universality or centricity that is presupposed in any semiotic-discursive order operates. Contemporary feminism as it is refracted through a politics of difference may be seen as responding to this challenge. In particular, the emergence of the category of difference has permitted feminist theory to investigate the materiality of the discursively interpellated female subject, and thereby to open up the significance of difference in embodiment for the politics of difference.

It is in this context that Mary John (1989, 63) makes the claim that "feminism is a politics before it is an epistemology—where questions of representation must deal with who speaks for whom as much as with what is being said."[1] These are, however, precisely epistemological questions. What can be argued is that a postmodern feminism, or one which is refracted through the politics of difference, is a feminism committed to a specific epistemological politics.

What follows is an attempt to characterize this epistemological politics. True to the spirit of this politics, this characterization is to be understood as historically contingent.

The Epistemological Orientation of Postmodern Feminist Theorizing

Contemporary postmodern feminist theorizing is characterized by the following epistemological orientations. Their symbiotic-oppositional relationship to dominant epistemological orientations will be evident as: 1. a deconstructive orientation to the modern and modernist theoretical traditions we inherit; 2. a post-universalistic mode of theorizing or, more accurately, the disruptive assertion of "minority" voices in respect of the inevitably universalistic aspects of theorizing; 3. a demonstration that binary constructions of difference not only specify a border that divides, but that this is simultaneously a border which unites, thus, an insistence on the instabilities and ambiguities of these constructions; 4. perspectivalism, which is a relational, not relativist, theory of knowledge (see Grosz, 1988, 100); 5. (a corollary of 4) the conception of acts of theorizing as historically contingent, and the acceptance thereby of disjunctive and conjunctural shifts and developments in theorizing; 6. an assumption of the significance of the positioning of the theorist(s) in relation to both institutionalized intellectual authority and to their actual and prospective audiences; 7. an assumption concerning the significance of the embodied subjectivity of the theorist(s); and 8. a conception of language as a "material, active, productive system" (Grosz, 1988, 100) and of theoretical debates as a language politics.

These orientations are emergent, and they are more or less explored at the level of self-conscious theorizing. None the less it is possible to say something about each of them.

1. A deconstructive relationship to the modernist traditions of theorizing that we have inherited. This relationship is one which has developed out of the dialectical interplay of reformist and separatist relationships of feminist theorizing to the modernist theoretical traditions. Reformist relationships were those that accepted the epistemological enterprise of a particular disciplinary tradition, and sought to reform its content by working on getting women and the world of women included. Separatist relationships assumed that these traditions were beyond repair, that they were irremediably inflected with the perspective and motivation of men as a social category committed to their gender dominance. Both these relationships have been disrupted within theoretical-political developments of the 1980s. Feminist theorists who sought to reform the theoretical enterprise, in my case, that of sociology, (Yeatman, 1990a; for philosophy, see Gatens, 1986) came to the conclusion that the nature of the enterprise was the problem, rather than specific lacunae or conceptualizations which could be corrected. In short, they brought themselves to the point of discerning the need for a paradigm change.

In this they might be thought to have come closer to separatist theoretical perspectives, except that these too became increasingly destabilized during the same period. The theoretical coherence of separatist perspectives depended on privileging the hierarchical difference between men and women above all other relationships of domination/difference, and on according "women" as an undifferentiated, same-gender/sex category a privileged ethical relationship to domination. In a sense, women in this framework assumed the mantle of the universal historical subject whose role it is to emancipate humankind from domination. In this case the emancipatory project was directed to only part of the universal humankind, women, because it was assumed that the other part was irremediably attached to a project of domination. This is an ethics of inversion, an unappealing orientation for those of us who are still oriented within an inclusive, emancipatory discourse, and it has come unstuck. Because this is an ethics of inversion, and works with its own version of binary oppositions, it is situated within a logos and politics of identity. Thus, it cannot survive the differentiation and dispersion of its core, privileged category: women. Yet this is what happened over the course of the 1980s as the many differences between women have been given voice, and, in particular, women who have been constituted as racially/ethnically other have discerned in the essentialist identity politics of women another version of "Western" universalizing and repression of difference. The privileging of gender difference/domination over class, race or ethnic difference/domination is unacceptable to women who are positioned as other in class, race or ethnic terms.[2]

Moreover, separatist perspectives in breaking the relationship with the theoretical traditions we have inherited suggested a false utopia of free, uncontaminated theoretical space. We cannot in some voluntaristic fashion break with these traditions. We have been formed by them as the binary logic of inversion in the separatist approach bears out. This is a particular type of complicity in discursive domination which reproduces the binary order of gender domination and thereby occludes the other axes of domination: race, ethnicity, language, age, (dis)ability (etc.).[3]

Clearly not all feminist theorists have abandoned separatist and reformist approaches to the theoretical traditions that we have inherited and which are institutionalized as the various disciplines of modern social science. This notwithstanding, the direction of contemporary theorizing is clear. It is to posit the phallocentric nature of the modernist intellectual enterprise, and to regard the possibilities of freedom from this enterprise (and its various versions) as requiring its radical critique. The conditions of this critique are identified with self-consciously using a perspective, which is perceived as constituted as other by the modernist enterprise, as the standpoint from which to interrogate it and bring its deep structures to light.

This perspective is feminism. It is a perspective adopted in awareness that those positioned as differently other will bring their own perspectives to bear on (de)constructing western modernist theory.

Moira Gatens (1986, 25, emphases in the original) brings out the significance of this feminist, deconstructive relationship to modernist theory, in this case philosophy:

> By *self-consciously* demonstrating that any philosophical paradigm is *not* neutral, these feminists make themselves, both as philosophers and women, *visible*. By making themselves visible, they in turn throw into question the legitimacy of claims and assumptions in philosophy that have been taken as axiomatic. In so far as this approach questions the very foundation and status of philosophy it also reveals the investments and concerns of philosophy. It does this by demonstrating not only *what is* excluded from a particular philosophy but also *why* it is crucial, for the very existence of that philosophy, to exclude it.

This statement of Gatens shows also that a feminist approach of theoretical deconstruction evinces unwillingness to evacuate the ground of knowledge production, to leave a particular discipline to its phallocentric leadership. Deconstruction, to paraphrase Gatens, makes feminists *visible* and *relevant* as social theorists.

2.   A post-universalistic approach to theorizing. Feminist theoretical approaches eschew the (illusory) archimedean point of the master subject surveying his universe. Because they adopt a perspectivalist and positioned relationship to theorizing, they accept the partiality and the specificity of their theoretical claims. This approach becomes further specified in the following five approaches.

3.   An insistence of the ambiguous nature of the border which constitutes difference. Feminist theoretical approaches reject the logic of identity by which the existence of something is self-presence. Self-presence is posited when the identity of something (a group, a nationality) is not simply established through positing its opposite. This is a necessary move in all identity games. The certainty of self-presence comes about through an additional maneuver: the dependency of the first term of identity on that which it excludes is completely invisibilized—and repressed. Feminist approaches insist on the return of this repression. They destabilize the identity of self-presence by representing what it excludes or opposes to itself. These approaches engage the ambiguities and instabilities of binary pairs. It turns out the border cannot be effectively policed. This is no less true of feminist versions of the dominant binary of phallocentric self-presence, where the privileged, now feminist, term of identity forgets/represses its dependence on what it has othered (the non-feminine).

Moreover feminist/postmodern models of differentiation tend to dispense with binary hierarchical models of difference (e.g. Western/Oriental; base/superstructure) and to substitute complex, multiple hierarchies of differentiation where ethnicity, race, gender and class mediate each other in specific, historically conjunctural modes. Binary, hierarchical differentiation thereby emerges as the essentialist, logocentric characteristic of any relationship of domination.

In respect of all the binaries in terms of which a phallocentric discursive order of domination operates (individual/society; nature/society; structure/agency, etc.), the first re-constructive inclination of current feminist theoretical approaches is to deal in terms of "and" rather than "or": for an exemplary and sophisticated expression of this see Donna Haraway's "Manifesto for Cyborgs" (1990). The sophistication of the "and" comes when, instead of accepting the two terms of a binarism as separate terms, they are posited as existing within each other. Trinh Minh-ha in her deconstruction of the Western model of individuated subjectivity which posits "self" in opposition, and thus in hierarchical relation to, "other," adopts an alternative conception of differentiation/individuation of subjectivity which exemplifies this approach. Here are two statements of hers:

> You said the other doesn't have to be very far away, it can be very close. Why not include this other within the self? Of course, as you said, one might still reproduce the model of opposition—but not necessarily if one opens the space to not representing, to difference, which is a notion that, when not reduced to a question of separation between entities, has the potential to undermine both hierarchy and opposition (1987, 145).

> The moment the insider steps out from the inside she's no longer a mere insider. She necessarily looks in from the outside while also looking out from the inside. Not quite the same, not quite the other, she stands in that undetermined threshold place where she constantly drifts in and out. Undercutting

that inside/outside opposition, her intervention is necessarily that of both not-quite an insider and not-quite an outsider. She is, in other words, this inappropriate other or same who moves about with always at least two gestures: that of affirming "I am like you" while persisting in her difference and that of reminding "I am different" while unsettling every definition of otherness arrived at (1988, 76).

This is an interpellated subject whose condition of being is the discursive space of "in-between" or, of "hybridized" identities. Thus, it is a subjectivity predicated on both complicity with dominant discursive formations and exclusion from them that characterizes the positionality of those who are discursively committed to developing the politics of difference. Annamarie Jagose's (1993) insightful treatment of the border as *both* "slash" and "suture" shows that hybridized identities cannot effect a synergy that goes beyond or transcends the border. Even if they could, this would be to reinstate a new border.

This approach has significant implications for how the binaries of nature/society, body/culture, subject/object, agency/structure and individual/society are deconstructed and alternatively approached within social science. For example, the exclusively constructivist approach to sex difference which posits socio-cultural forces as constructing what sex difference becomes in a social context is one which depends on the theoretical binarism of nature and culture (society). Such constructivism accords culture (society) status as the unmarked term, allowing it an undetermined degree of freedom with regard to the marked term: "nature." This permits those who are positioned as exponents of the freedom of culture/society to arbitrate what embodied sex difference is to mean in social-cultural-technical terms *even when* they do not share the embodied sex in question.

Thus bio-medical reproductive technologies are designed and operationalized by men within a phallocentric discursive order for women. The whole picture shifts if we adopt the theoretical approach of Trinh Minh-ha, and permit sex difference ("nature") and gender ("society/culture") to be two terms, each of which exists both inside and outside the other.

    4. A perspectivalist theory of knowledge. All knowledge is situated knowledge, and is governed by the perspective of those who are the knowers. These perspectives are irreducibly multiple and interdiscursive in character. Since the subjectivity/positioning of the knowers is historically variable and specific, the perspectivalist base of knowledge renders all knowledges historically specific: "by the affirmation of its own perspectivism, the fact that theories elaborate particular points of view, specific aims and values, it [feminist theory] accepts its own historicity" (Grosz, 1988, 100). This is not a limitation because there is no alternative, and clearly "we" can come to understand a great deal about the historical variability and differences of subjectivity by investigating the knowledge in which it is inscribed, even when our access to these knowledges is necessarily mediated through our perspective. Again Trinh Minh-ha's insider-in-the-outsider/outsider-in-the-insider trope is suggestive for what we may do with subjectivities in relation to which we are positioned as historically and/or culturally other.

As Grosz (1988, 100) points out, a situationalist, perspectivalist theory of knowledge entails a relational theory of knowledge. This is not the same thing as relativism. In the context of discussing a feminist perspectivism, Grosz (1988, 100) clarifies the distinction between these: theory "occupies a position (that of the sexed subject) and is connected to other practices, rather than, in relativism, having no fixed position." This means that theory is "neither neutral nor indifferent to individual particularities (as the objectivist or absolutist maintains), nor purely free-floating, a position any subject can occupy at will (as the subjectivist or relativist maintains)."

A relational theory of knowledge posits an historically specific conjuncture of positioned knowledges and of their imbrication. This conjuncture may be said to be the historical pragmatics of knowledge and knowledge production for a specific temporal/spatial discursive universe or linked series of such universes. It is evident that there is nothing chaotic in the sense of random or free-floating about this picture. There is no site available to knowers outside the specific conjuncture of positioned knowledges they inhabit.

5.   *An approach to theorizing as an historically specific and contingent activity.* Social theorizing can be situated within different historicities, where within the same unit of time (a year or decade) different subjects are positioned within distinct and different historical trajectories or what Mani (1989, 5) calls "different temporalities of struggle." Their theorizing will be accordingly specific and different. For example, the social theorizing of postcolonials within the Pacific-Asia Basin has a different, albeit partially connected, historicity than that of those positioned as metropolitan social theorists in the Trans-Atlantic and Western European societies. Moreover, the "same" social theorist may be historically positioned as a knowing subject in varying and sometimes radically varying ways depending on her situatedness in the politics of location (Mani, 1989, 5). In the same degree her theoretical productions may be more or less disjunctive in respect of each other.

It will be seen that this approach does not encourage the grand, integrative systems-building efforts of a Talcott Parsons or Jürgen Habermas, who attempt to synthesize modern social theory. Instead it radicalizes Weber's (1949) distinction between "genetic" and "generic" concepts or aspects of theorizing. By "genetic" concepts, Weber was referring to the specificity of the object as our values and standards of relevance lead us to construct it as an object for study. This specificity is historical. This is why Weber calls the object as it is constructed by the social/cultural scientist (the "ideal type") an "historical individual." These historical individuals account for the basic substance of what it is we are doing when we are engaging in social theorizing.

There are also "generic" concepts. By these, Weber (1949, 100) is referring to our use for limited heuristic purposes of class concepts, "which merely summarize the common features of certain empirical phenomena," for example, what Weber presupposed to be the common features of economic exchange.

At first sight, something like this idea of generic concepts appears useful. There are ways in which we want to be able to use the concept "political" across the historically very distinct social theories of Aristotle, Locke and Touraine. However, Weber's empiricist conception of the "class concept" will not do. If we can appropriate a class concept of "political" it is because it belongs to a generic discourse of the political as this discourse has been reinvented and maintained as a tradition within the discursive self-production of "Western civilization." In short, these class concepts are also "historical individuals," but their status as such within discourse at a civilizational level accords them a generic status in contrast to the intra-civilizational specificity of genetic concepts.

This I take to be the burden of a good deal of what Marilyn Strathern (1988) is doing in her book, *The Gender of the Gift*. In that book, while she reiterates the point that our "class concepts," like exchange-economies, gift-economies, public, domestic, political, ritual and so on, are the analytic concepts of modern western social science, and are not those of the Melanesian societies she and other Melanesianists study, she is clear that we have nothing else but these concepts. Thus, the access of the Melanesianist to "indigenous" concepts is refracted through those concepts' difference from his/her (social scientist's) "analytic" concepts. This does not prevent the social scientist's use of "indigenous" concepts to make them self-conscious of their own "analytic" concepts. In so doing, Strathern is able to show both that Hageners do not devalue household (domestic) production in relation to political gift exchange, and that "we" (Westerners) do devalue domestic production in relation to economic (market-mediated) exchange.

What Strathern does not investigate is what may happen when "indigenous" postcolonial anthropologies, in particular, and social sciences, in general, develop. Perhaps she presupposes that when erstwhile natives stop being the objects and become the subjects of social science, this perforce requires their acculturation into the discursive order of (modernist) social science. This is undoubtedly true on one level, given the metropolitan organization and political dynamics of modern social science. However, we are likely to see the emergence of historically specific points of confrontation and deconstruction on the part of postcolonial social scientists in relation to "our" (and this must include western feminist) concepts. These confrontations may destabilize our class concepts in a way that "we" simply cannot manage to achieve ourselves. Consider what may be the consequences if "indigenous" concepts are made the basis of a perspective on western social science by those who are positioned as "indigenous" subjects for western master-subject conceptions of "the economic" (for a non-indigenous, hybridized Western/postcolonial, white New Zealander feminist perspective on the economic, see Waring, 1988). This brings us to the sixth point of approach in feminist theorizing.

6. *The significance of the theorist's positioning in respect of the institutional bases of intellectual authority.* In a presentation on "legacies of critical practice in the 1980s," Silvia Kolbowski (in Foster, 1987, 102–103) comments on an earlier presentation in the same series by Douglas Crimp (Foster, 1987, 31–38), in which he positioned himself as a gay art critic who seeks to make visible the strategies of public address in exhibitions which marginalize gay people and gay issues. In a following discussion of the issues raised in the presentations, Kolbowski (in Foster, 1987, 108) addresses Crimp: "I'm not saying one can't speak with conviction or one can't be accusatory. I'm saying one has to take into account the discourses one employs, and there was nothing in your [Crimp's] presentation that really acknowledged your position as critic and historian."

Later, Kolbowski (Foster, 1987, 109) poses a very tricky question: "What, in his presentation, would make us question Douglas's authority?" A tricky question indeed for those of us who wear like a velvet glove the institutional authority of academe.

This is an important question for feminist theorists who understand their relationship to social theorizing to be a self-empowering relationship. It would be a serious contradiction if their modes of self-empowerment de-authorized the voice of less credentialed feminists, and non-feminist others. What Kolbowski appears to be calling for is something which is implied in feminist approaches to theorizing: an accountability of the theorist to her readers, students and other audiences, through making her positioning open to question by these audiences. Engagement in a commitment to accountability in these terms positions readers, students and other audiences as interlocutors in relation to the work at hand. They become active participants, rather than passive audiences in the event, and thereby turn the event into a process. In this context, then, accountability, like all forms of political accountability, contributes to the forming of theoretical "publics."

Accountability is a difficult value to practice, because, given the Western dualism of subject and object and the Western commitment to an "impersonal" mode of theoretical speech, it is easily appropriated as a "confessional speech" rather than as an integral part of the academic/public discourse. Again the interchange involving Douglas Crimp's presentation and Silvia Kolbowski's challenge to it is instructive. In responding to Kolbowski's challenge, Crimp (Foster, 1987, 108) says among other things: "To clarify my position I need to talk about the response to my [original] statement [as a self-positioned gay interlocutor of dominant heterosexual aesthetic practices]. There was very little response at the time, but what I heard afterward reflected the general feeling that when a gay person speaks from an explicitly gay position it is taken to be a confessional speech."

Later, this is followed by a most insightful comment by Craig Owens (in Foster, 1987, 110–112):

> One of the things I also heard in your [Kolbowski's] talk is the necessity not to accept certain unified "I's", the necessity to deconstruct notions of identity or the places from which we speak as given to us institutionally. Now the identity of the gay man is an institutionally prescribed phenomenon—it is largely constructed by medical and legal discourses. And one has to question that position when one want [sic] to address issues as a gay man....Otherwise it becomes a self-referential discourse—to say who I am before I speak. That's also why it tends to be perceived as "coming out" when one doesn't question that identity.

The point Owens is making here is an important one. Positionality cannot be declared in advance. To attempt this is to thrust a politics of positionality back into the confessional modes of accountability of the bourgeois sovereign self. A politics of positionality—and the accountability it enjoins for specific subjects—is specified in terms of the dialogical, rhetorical practices which open up in any particular discursive terrain. How developed this politics may be depends on commitments to democratizing rhetorical practice, commitments which proceed from discursive struggles themselves.

Crimp has different discursive options about the way to operate within his positionality. In order to make the perspectivalism of his contribution and its relationship to an historical-political pragmatics of knowledge clear, he has to invoke his positionality. He can do this in ways that open up the discursive space to other voices of difference or he can do it in ways that foreclose this space. With the former option he implicitly invites those who are insiders to explore the outsiders within themselves: this engenders an open-ended process of discursive reflexivity about the positionality of the subjects who participate in the process. It is very likely that this process will change their position. With the latter option he addresses insiders as those whose position excludes him. Since closure is the starting point of this meeting, the insiders are left with nothing to do except to acknowledge their complicity in past, present and future exclusions of gay outsiders. That this constitutes a discursive game of reciprocal confession which actually confirms the binarism of exclusion and inclusion should be evident.

Kolbowski is suggesting one way that the option which represents the opening up of polyphonal exploration of positionalities might have been taken up by Crimp. Crimp might have said something like the following: *I want to address you as a gay man who perceived the co-sequential staging of The New AIDS Show and the Hans Haacke exhibition at the New Museum as being done in such a way as to segregate the former, and thus the issues of gay people, from the latter, an explicitly political work.*[4] *Now how do I do this? I can address you as fellow aesthetes, art critics and academics. My address then is one of a Puritan's berating of his impure colleagues, and it operates to confirm our shared status as elite gatekeepers of aesthetic values.[5] Perhaps I cannot problematize the issue of the relationship of those two exhibitions to gay publics, unless you and I—"we" even—problematize the issue of how we as aesthetes and critics construct publics. Do we construct publics at all? Or do we construct "audiences" who are positioned in such ways that they cannot enter into the process of becoming and discovering themselves as a public (or series of publics)? So how do I pose to you an issue of exclusion in which I have a direct interest to you? How do we explore whether in our discursive practices we are constructing audiences or publics? And who do we work with to do this?*

The positioning of the feminist/postmodernist theorist, then, is one which in principle is politically accountable to those who are positioned as constituting the context of and potential audiences for her work. The principle of accountability can be elaborated to develop into "strategies of public address" (Foster, 1987, 31–55), where these evoke or connect up with publics for whom her work may be relevant.

7.   *The significance of embodied subjectivity for feminist theorizing.* A number of feminist theorists (Grosz, 1989; Gatens, 1988; Landes, 1988; Pateman, 1988) have argued that the formal universals of bourgeois political theory are in fact "sexed" universals which express a phallocentric political order and the exclusion of women. These critiques eschew strategies of retaining a formal universal ideal while seeking to correct for its particularistic excesses. Instead, they reject formal universals and insist on the significance of embodied differences in respect of sex, sexuality and, it would follow, life-cycle stages.

The basic proposition here is that if there is to be a vision of freedom which contests phallocentricism, it must admit the existence and the significance of the particularity of embodied subjects. This means admitting the differences between differently embodied subjects. These differences are not reducible to a simple dimorphic sex difference, nor are they without socio-cultural mediation.

Admission of the particularity of embodied subjectivity involves the rejection of the fundamental mind/body dualism which is inscribed in modern social science. Such admission depends on providing the discursive space in which differently embodied subjects themselves can find their own voices regarding their differences as embodied subjects.

To date this is unexplored territory, although there is theoretical preparation for such exploration in the theoretical traditions of psychoanalysis, especially the Lacanian-psychoanalytic feminist theorizing of Irigaray, Kristeva and Le Doeuff (Grosz, 1989). In principle, exploration of this territory opens up the social ecologies of embodied subjectivity, where these social ecologies involve not only the specific social-psychoanalytic-material histories of particular subjects but the linkages of these histories to shared and wider social, ecological histories of urban environments, material cultures of food production and consumption, physique and physical exercise, architecture and its relationship to "natural" environments, and so on.

For social theory, if embodied subjectivity is to be accorded significance, it must find a way into accounts of the positioning of theorists and their interlocutors. Among other things, the implications of this are that analyses of high-tech cultures or environments do not proceed independently of the analyst's positioning in relation to these cultures or environments. Gender may or may not be of particular significance here. Of more significance may be the analyst's normal habitat. The world is seen differently from an affluent, high-rise, high-tech apartment in New York City than it is from a semi-urban, wood-heated house outside Amherst in Massachusetts.

8. *The significance of language.* Feminist/postmodern theorizing has insisted on the non-neutrality of language and discourse, and has made the politics of language and discourse central to the processes of theoretical critique and theory construction. The effect of this is to make all concepts potentially into what William Connolly calls "contestable concepts," and to require the exposition of a concept to be an exposition of its political discursive history.

When language is not regarded as a neutral medium of theoretical propositions and empirical observation but is regarded instead as constitutive of these propositions and observations, works of social science become "texts." As texts they can be analyzed in relation to their contexts (intertextuality), and to the discourses of which they are operational units (see Kress, 1985, chapter 1).

An important aspect of the context of a text is the multiple discursive positionings of the subjects who hear or read the text. They engage in multiple readings of the text, and it depends on the discursive politics of a text as to whether it accords legitimacy to these multiple readings or seems to invite only one "correct" reading. Certain discourses, for example econometric expressions of neo-classical economics, function to effect discursive closure, that is, to bracket out the legitimacy and even existence of alternative economic discourses. Certain modes of arguing discursive claims effect closure by sealing off the genre from alternative ways of constructing the phenomenon in hand. For example, many textbooks for introductory sociology conform to the conventions of a genre which presents concepts in the form of a definition (of anomie, mode of production, etc.), where the discursive political history of the concept is bracketed out (foreclosed). Scientistic modes of argument which privilege statistical genres often function in a similar way.

The connection of the significance accorded language to the accountability of the positioning of social theorists will be evident. Deconstruction of the language of a text which, for example, surfaces the phallocentric features of the Marxian concept of labor (see Klein, 1989) not only indicates something about Marx's positioning as a social theorist. It operates also as an invitation to those who find themselves positioned in ways that the text does not seem to authorize, to explore and to contest this exclusion.

Concluding Remarks

The epistemological politics of postmodern feminist theorizing is an emergent politics which is finding its way into the social and cultural sciences. At this stage it is an under-specified politics. Much of the contemporary contribution to this politics comprises agenda-setting rather than elaboration of agendas already enunciated. This piece is to be understood as bridging these agenda-setting and agenda-elaboration stages.

2

Postmodern Epistemological Politics and Social Science

Postmodernism is a contested zone. However, many and maybe most commentators agree that it represents a crisis of authority for the western knowing subject, posed by the refusal to stay silenced on the part of those whom this subject had cast as Other: natives, colonials, women and all who are placed in a client relationship to expert, professional authority. By insisting on their own voice and status as subjects, these erstwhile objects of modern western knowledge have disrupted the epistemological order of domination inscribed within modern, western knowledge. They have caused a major crisis of legitimacy for this order, while, simultaneously, there has been a series of strategies mounted by the gatekeepers of modern social science to maintain both its authority and its ongoing license to assert itself as subject over those placed as object to its knowing gaze.

Postmodernism, then, can be interpreted from the standpoint of what I shall call the master subject contemplating the issues of legitimacy for his authority which arise from the refusal of those cast as other to stay silent. Or, it can be interpreted from the standpoint of those who are placed as the disruptive and challenging voices of the Other.

It is important to recognize that postmodernism is quite different depending on which of these standpoints is adopted. For the former, postmodernism is a general sea-change, reflecting the combined impacts of various social, cultural and technological changes. The revolt of the Other is acknowledged in an over-generalized, abstract way. It remains unspecified and uninvestigated. It is immediately drowned within an acknowledgment of the increasingly globalized context of social science, and a reinstatement of the social scientist's authority as "observer" of these general patterns and dynamics of change.

From the standpoint of those who are contesting their status as Other, postmodernism appears as the efforts of the modern imperial, patriarchal master subject to manage the extent and direction of the crisis for his authority. Postcolonial and antiracist intellectuals such as Edward Said and Cornel West (see West, 1988 and 1989), respectively, quite evidently view postmodernism as without any emancipatory dynamics of its own: it is "reaction" of the kind that seeks to preempt and coopt. It is a reaction which accommodates by depoliticizing the challenges to the order of the modern master subject (see Said, 1989, 222–223). Indeed, the silence of contemporary social science on post-war liberation movements, on the way that they have interpellated and cross-referenced each other, and on the way that they have undertaken as a fundamental strategy the contestation of colonized subjectivities, has been deafening. I refer here not only to the various national liberation and anti-colonial movements but to the women's, gay and black liberation movements within the metropolitan and semi-metropolitan national contexts.

The relationship of feminism to postmodernism is more complex. Contemporary feminist theorists working within the politics of difference are making postmodernism over to their own agendas. Postcolonial and feminist theorists of difference converge, however, in their insistence on a nexus between knowledge and power, and in their sustained contestation of how this nexus works to maintain and reproduce domination within modern social science. It is necessary to say something of the epistemological politics they espouse. In so saying, I am constructing an ideal-type of this politics which would be evidenced to more or less extent by those who could be reasonably regarded as postcolonial and feminist theorists of difference. It is evidenced most in the work of feminist theorists of difference who are either also situated as postcolonials (e.g., John, 1989 and Mani, 1989), or as "living on borders and in margins" in respect of two or more cultures. The phrase comes from Gloria Anzaldua, a lesbian Chicana who grew up on the border of (US) New Mexico and Mexico:

> The actual physical borderland that I'm dealing with in this book is the Texas-U.S. Southwest/Mexican border. The psychological borderlands, the sexual borderlands and the spiritual borderlands are not particular to the Southwest. In fact, the Borderlands are physically present wherever two or more cultures edge each other, where people of different races occupy the same territory, where under, lower, middle and upper classes touch, where the space between two individuals shrinks with intimacy (1987, Preface).

Oppositional Intellectuals and Their Critique of Epistemological Foundationalism

These oppositional intellectuals agree with what is arguably the core feature of postmodernism: the critique of epistemological foundationalism. Put simply, this critique is based in a rejection of mirror theories of knowledge, where knowledge, if it is to be true or accurate knowledge, mirrors an order of being outside itself (see Rorty, 1979). In such accounts of knowledge, all that matters is that the knower is trained correctly to use the techniques and methods which permit him direct, "objective" access to reality. These techniques and methods combine experimental or quasi-experimental modes of empirical investigation with logical rigor. The experimental orientation presupposes that knowledge claims are testable in some sense in relation to a reality which is external to the knower, and which the knower thereby encounters as a facticity he must respect. The logical criterion of truth or accuracy presupposes the existence of universal reason in that it assumes that logical modeling by its own preferably mathematical precision is self-evidently true. Such a truth claim depends on a metaphysical assumption concerning the existence of universal reason.

A rationalist metaphysics of this kind turns out to be a rationalist version of the divine right of kings. The rationalism ensures a particular authority to intellectuals as the rational knowers of reality. Since they can discern the laws of social-historical being, it is their knowledge which is to provide the rational basis for the law and policy of governments. All putatively objective knowledge acquires the authority of such access to being. Their science permits them "objective" knowledge of the nature of those who are subjected to government. They thereby assume the authority of modern professionals who know the real needs of laypersons better than these people do themselves. Thus, the scientific revolutionary who designs a political project based on the real as distinct from the false (i.e. "expressed") needs of the people is no different in this respect from the profession of doctors who understand their expertise as authorizing them to discern the real as distinct from the expressed needs of their patients. We can see here how the authority of a foundationalist science ensures that the voice of the scientists not only prevails over but silences all those who are not scientists.

Moreover, this monocultural rationalism not only maintains a clear distinction between those who legitimately wear the authority of science and those who cannot do so, but ensures very clear membership rules for access to the club of scientists. The authority of a foundationalist science constitutes the scientist as Subject to all those who, brought under the regime of the scientist's observation, are constituted as Object. They are objectified *in order to* produce the subjectivity of the scientist surveying the universe.

This means that individuals who belong to groups which are consistently objectified by modern science—women, blacks, colonials, peasants and other groups typified as stupid, prejudiced or ignorant—are admitted to the scientific club only as exceptions to the norm for their group. There is a price for their admission: assimilation. They are admitted to the club of scientists only if they combine an appropriate training in the procedures of foundationalist science with the adoption of the *persona* of the rational sovereign subject. In adopting this *persona*, "minority group" scientists are always to place loyalty to "the" community of scientists over loyalty to their origins. However, if on occasion they should contravene the scientific norms of disembodied, detached proceduralism and commit an emotional excess of some kind, this will be forgiven as an inevitable flaw which confirms their status as somewhat less than real scientists—as subaltern scientists. The flaw is even required. That is, subaltern scientists are allowed to orient their science in terms of values which pertain to their origins, as long as these values are not elaborated so as to call into question and to politicize the scientific enterprise itself.

Feminist and postcolonial intellectuals who refuse to be assimilated on these terms place themselves in a contestatory relationship to the authority of modern, foundationalist science. Because they do so, it is obvious from the standpoint of modern foundationalist science, that they are not proper scientists. Hence, as far as social science goes, their contestation and knowledge claims are consigned to the soft, discursive world of the humanities, or to the post-disciplinary nether worlds of Cultural Studies, Women's Studies, Black Studies, etc.[1]

Feminist and postcolonial intellectuals develop a critique of foundationalist theories of knowledge. They adopt the Nietzschean/Foucauldian proposition that we know reality only *via* our representations of reality. These representations are not simply historically and culturally variable, or, rather, their multiplicity reflects difference in representational perspective. This difference arises out of differences in the *positioning* of knowing subjects in relation to the historicity of interconnected relationships of domination and contestation.

This idea of positioning is both relational and political: the positioning of a knowing subject is located within the time-and-space specific politics of particular relationships of contested domination. Thus, this perspectivalist account of knowledge is to be distinguished from pluralist accounts of culturally relative knowledge. Where the latter maintain the ideological fiction of a horizontally integrated community of differently value-oriented intellectuals, post-foundationalist accounts deal in a politics of knowledge where principles of vertical integration are challenged but not supplanted by those of horizontal integration.

In short, where feminist and postcolonial intellectuals proceed beyond cultural relativism is in their insistence on contested representations within what are putatively singular or common cultures. They refuse to accord a discursive formation coherence through any other effects than those of power, of domination. Feminist theorists carry over this idea into an account of their own identity as positioned subjects. Indeed, precisely because women are positioned as Other to the integrity of the masculine subject, they are not required, nor do their circumstances readily permit, a sense of their own subjective identity as an integral, bounded, coherent entity (see de Lauretis, 1990). For feminist intellectuals still measuring their identity and worth in relation to the master subject's integrity, this appears—just as the master subject has always said—as a lack (lack of maturity, lack of development in respect of the higher levels of social and ethical life). However, this project of "seeking assimilation and a place for women within hegemonic discourse, within 'the ideology of the same'" (de Lauretis, 1990, 132) has been displaced by a feminist politics of difference informed by a postfoundationalist epistemology.

It will be clear that these oppositional intellectuals also refuse the effect of cultural integrity that an uncritical acceptance of national or local boundaries generates, an effect on which the idea of a collective conscience depends. Instead they insist on the interconnections between the ways national, class, gender, race and ethnic differences are produced and reinvented in order to maintain and expand a globally integrated network of relationships of domination. This is a series of networks rather than a closed system, an historically contingent socio-cultural-economic formation, which looks and operates differently depending on where one is positioned within it (see Haraway, 1988). To the degree that the system is contingently integrated through techniques of discursive management, these operate to distinguish those positioned as the international elite of managers of this system and those positioned as the objects and instruments of their regime. The mainstream social sciences provide the intellectual foundations of this system of global management.

Feminist and postcolonial intellectuals thereby enjoin a *politics* of representation. Central to this politics is the twofold strategic question: whose representations prevail? who has the authority to represent reality? To put the question differently: who must be silenced in order that these representations prevail? whose voice is deprived of authority so that they may prevail? This is a politics of representation which insists on the material effects of discursive power, and which contextualizes the institutional politics of the Western university within the world-historical dynamics of Western capitalist-patriarchal-imperial domination and its contestation.

This is a representational politics which refuses legitimacy to the consensual community of rational scientists which both Karl Popper and Jürgen Habermas invoke in their respective conceptions of science and rational discourse. Feminist and postcolonial intellectuals make visible the structure of domination on which the "we-ness" of that community, and the possibility of such consensus, are dependent. In short, they show how the consensus depends on the systematic exclusion of those who would dissent if they were given voice, which they are not.

Feminist and postcolonial intellectuals are clearly attempting to open up contested epistemological spaces. Theirs is a narrative which is ordered by metaphors of struggle, contest, forced closure, strategic interventions, and contingent opening of public spaces for epistemological politics. There is no illusion that, just because the dominant epistemological order is subject to contest, the material force of this dominant order will not prevail. After all, the dominant epistemological order is inscribed in the material institutions and relationships of modern capitalism and imperialism. In this context, the response of master subjects who recognize the crisis of authority, and who recommend the development of non-foundationalist, intellectual "conversation" is a familiar liberal's attempt to get the raucous and dangerous mobs off the streets by tempting some of their leaders into safely cloistered, polite conversation in civilized comfort with the decision-making elite.

By disrupting the we-ness of the community of knowers and locating all knowledge claims within the politics of contested domination, the epistemological force of the politics of difference is to refuse any vantage point for knowledge outside or beyond this field of contested domination. There is no place outside an ideological positioning within this field, and there can be no innocence in respect to how knowledge claims enter into the politics of modern capitalist-patriarchal-imperial domination.

Edward Said indicates the way in which this must mean an ongoing crisis for the discipline of anthropology, situated as it is as the knowledge discipline which has informed and legitimized the modern western project of civilization/colonization on a world-system scale. As he points out, this is a crisis not simply for those stages of anthropology which represent its service to the colonial regimes of direct and indirect rule. If, in the era of independent statehood, anthropology no longer serves this kind of colonial governmentality, it still serves western empire by continuing to exoticise, to "other," non-western peoples—not least by representing them as legitimate objects for the scientific gaze of the western observer. Said's (1989, 212) insistence on "the problematic of the observer" is crucial:

> Look at the many pages of the very brilliantly sophisticated argument in the works of the metatheoretical [anthropological] scholars, or in Sahlins and Wolf, and you will begin perhaps suddenly to note how someone, an authoritative, explorative, elegant, learned voice, speaks and analyzes, amasses evidence, theorizes, speculates about everything—except itself. Who speaks? For what and to whom?

The problematic of the observer allows us to see how modern social science constructs the object of the observer's gaze so as to make it appear that the observer has nothing to do with the dynamics of the object itself. When those who are objectified for the purposes of modern social science speak, their voices are heard not as interlocutors placed within a shared field of dialogical contestation and negotiation with the social scientists. Instead their voices are maintained as voices of the object by being treated as further evidence to be studied by the social scientist who keeps his identity firmly outside this objectified and subordinated community (see Fabian, 1983). As Said (1989, 219) puts it: "The Western Africanists read African writers as source material for their research, Western Middle East specialists treat Arab or Iranian texts as primary evidence for their research, while the direct, even importunate solicitations of debate and intellectual engagement from the formerly colonized are left largely unattended."

Subaltern Intellectuals and the Politics of Intellectual Authority

The crucial epistemological shift for postfoundationalist, critical social science concerns its entering into the politics of intellectual authority. In so doing it can build on an earlier tradition of critical social theory, a sociology of the knowledge producers—the intellectuals—as the new class (Gouldner, 1979; Konrad and Szelenyi, 1979). New class theory enquires into how the interest of the knowledge-producer as a knowledge-producer impacts on knowledge (Szelenyi and Martin, 1988, 649). It attributes a distinctive interest to intellectuals as monopolists of cultural capital in both the conservation of this monopoly, and in the extension of the capacity of cultural capital to translate into money capital and political capital. Where new class theory maintains a marxist (materialist) exteriority of the class's interest to its ideology (knowledge in this case), post-foundationalist critical theory insists on the mutually constitutive character of this relationship. Intellectuals are constituted precisely through the relationship of knowledge-producers to those who are the objects of knowledge, and, thus, insofar as they enter the domain of knowledge, are produced by knowledge. This relationship *is* the cultural capital of the intelligentsia.

Put differently, it is this relationship which constitutes the authority of the intellectual. As a general rule, the politics of intellectual authority concerns its maintenance as an unproblematic expression of objective, foundationalist knowledge, on the one hand; and the various challenges to such an account of knowledge which insist on its constitutive, value-ridden, interested and political characteristics. Within earlier epistemological debates concerning the politics of intellectual authority, positivism has expressed the resistance among mainstream intellectuals to the politicization of their bid for power, while anti-positivism has expressed the variously oriented intellectual challenges to positivistic renditions of intellectual authority as objective science (see e.g. Adorno et al., 1976).

Subaltern intellectuals are those who are admitted into the class of intellectuals on just the same terms that women have been educated to make good wives and mothers, and colonials have been educated to rule on behalf of the metropolis within the colonies: namely, as intellectuals whose authority as intellectuals is qualified by, and indeed subjected to, their lack of authority in being positioned as subordinates. Because subaltern intellectuals are those who are refused entry to the New Class elites, and to the ruling levels of the institutions which gatekeep intellectual authority, they are tempted to regard themselves as unable to claim New Class cultural capital even if they want to. However, it is clear they are constituted as bearers of cultural capital in relation to their own subaltern constituencies, namely the non-intellectual Others with whom they are identified as women and/or postcolonials. They are thereby vertically integrated into a stratified system of cultural capital and accorded the role of mediating and domesticating the claims of these constituencies by turning them into intellectualized claims subject to techniques of rational administration. This happens, for example, when postcolonial intellectuals are inducted into Western development theory and when feminist western intellectuals theorize "women's" claims in ways that make them subject to legal adjudication and public policy.

Vertical integration of this kind is destabilized when the subaltern intellectuals simultaneously surrender illusions of upward mobility within the stratified system of cultural capital *and* discover the power of horizontal ties among themselves. Such horizontality tables difference of positioning amongst subaltern intellectuals, and forces them into an empirical awareness of their different perspectivally-oriented knowledges, differences that cannot be "resolved" by being subsumed within some transcendent ideal of a scientific community. The current politics of representation which postcolonial feminists and "women of color" have opened up in respect of what they have perspectivally constituted as the limited and interested ideology of "Western" feminism is a case in point (see Haraway, 1988; Ong, 1988; and Mohanty, 1988).

The Contradictory Relationship of Subaltern Intellectuals to Intellectual Authority

Subaltern intellectuals are positioned in a contradictory relationship to intellectual authority. As intellectuals, and as evidenced especially when they are directing their intellectual claims upwards as it were, to the ruling elites of academe, they are drawn within the culture of intellectual authority and use its conventions unproblematically. At the same time, as subaltern intellectuals, they are not only positioned as outsiders in respect of these ruling elites, which can foster a tendency to call into question the reliance of these elites for their status on intellectual authority, but they are positioned with loyalties and ties both to fellow subaltern intellectuals who lack access to the institutionalized capital of the New Class, and to subaltern non-intellectuals.

Thus, when a subaltern intellectual, who is well-credentialed in terms of levels and kinds of degrees and in terms of academic appointments, publication access, and networks, publishes an oppositional piece within a mainstream, elite journal, this is communication upwards. Accordingly, even if it eschews an objectivist (foundationalist) epistemology, it is likely to be dressed up in the arcane, technically precise, esoteric language of the intellectual elite. The privilege of this elite may be recognized by there being no requirement of its members to communicate with anyone outside the elite: thus, the highest circles of the metropolitan Academy are insulated from the *demos,* namely anyone less initiated than the brightest Ph.D. aspirants among the graduate students.

While there can be no doubt that technically precise language permits certain types of ratiocination impossible without it, and intellectual knowledge would be deprived of insight and depth without these, the subaltern intellectual is one who is positioned as having actually to accord status to that familiar question— why can't you put your ideas in language which ordinary people can understand? This is because the subaltern intellectual is positioned across audiences. Her audiences comprise not just those who may arbitrate and foster her academic career, but women who want to be introduced to university-based feminist ideas in order to become, not necessarily graduate students in Women's Studies, but the kinds of service-delivery practitioners they want to be, as well as women within the general community. Moreover, she may be placed in significant peer relationships with Black and/or postcolonial feminist intellectuals who either cannot get access to the Academy and its publication institutions, or who choose to maintain communicational links with their own constituencies, for example, women who share their non-intellectual "origins," in ways which require different types of publication outlet. bell hooks (1984, 15), for example, is an important Black, feminist theorist in the U.S., who refuses to use esoteric language and who publishes her work through a non-academic, politically oriented press. To be sure, she has an academic position in a good liberal arts college, but her positioning operates to orient her as an oppositional intellectual seeking to communicate with Black women, and to contest the implicit racism of white, western feminism, as is evident in this statement:

> It is essential for continued feminist struggle that black women recognize the special vantage point our marginality gives us and make use of this perspective to criticize the dominant racist, classist, sexist hegemony as well as to envision and create a counter-hegemony. I am suggesting that we have a central role to play in the making of feminist theory and a contribution to offer that is unique and valuable. The formation of a liberatory feminist theory and praxis is a collective responsibility, one that must be shared. Though I criticize aspects of feminist movement as we have known it so far, a critique which is sometimes harsh and unrelenting, I do so not in an attempt to diminish feminist struggle but to enrich, to share in the work of making a liberatory ideology and a liberatory movement.

Monocultural rationalists who maintain the idea of the possibility of a neutral, non-positioned, non-perspectivalist knowledge, perceive the contemporary politics of representation as threatening the very idea of science. As indeed is the case if by science is meant a foundationalist conception of knowledge and its procedures, namely an orientation to "truth," Post-foundationalist knowledge surrenders this orientation, but it is still science in the sense of objectifying for its purposes whatever is deemed to come under its ambit. How the objectification proceeds is subject to a politics of method. This notwithstanding, such objectification is subject to reflective evidential and logical procedures which by their adoption distinguish the scientist from the non-scientist.

This point is worth laboring because both foundationalist and post-foundationalist scientists too readily participate in a game where the former get to wear the mantle of "science" and the latter the mantle of "politics." This permits the former to complacently insulate themselves in the face of the threat the latter represent. Perhaps more dangerously it permits the latter to smuggle into their post-foundationalist intellectual claims a moral species of foundationalism. Their claims are right because they are more virtuous, more in line with contemporary standards of justice.[2] This is a righteousness almost impossible to abjure by those intellectuals who are positioned as marginals within the Academy.

As to scientific methods of objectification, if postfoundationalist intellectuals must as intellectuals adopt these methods, their positioning makes it likely that some among their audiences will question their observer role. That is to say, the problematic of the observer becomes an open problematic for these oppositional intellectuals: they cannot escape or evade it. This injects a tension into their intellectual work, a tension that produces a vulnerability to demands for accountability of their work to non-academic intellectuals and to non-intellectual audiences. For these intellectuals, there are unresolved tensions between demands for accountability to the academic authorities for the quality of the academic performance their work represents, and demands for accountability to the subaltern constituencies in which their politics is entailed.

It is common for foundationalist intellectuals to reject post-foundationalist knowledge politics for its inevitable subscription to and complicity with the nature of intellectual authority.[3] Postfoundationalist intellectuals, as those who embrace an open politics of representation, are vulnerable to this kind of charge only if and when they deny it. It is too much to expect that the contradictions and tensions in their positioning will not operate sometimes (often?) to encourage such denial. Nonetheless, there is an emergent postfoundationalist epistemology which is oriented in terms of the premise that knowledge claims are irresolvably multiple, and comprise historically specified fields of contested claims. As knowledge, these claims have no more status than the historicity of their discursive positioning.

No amount of good intentions, then, will obviate the post-foundationalist, as the foundationalist, intellectual's assertion of the domination which is inscribed in the knowing subject/object relationship. What distinguishes the post-foundationalist from the foundationalist intellectual is the former's positioning within a contradictory pull of demands for accountability, some of which both problematize and challenge her use of the intellectual's authority.

Acceptance of these types of demands for accountability cannot rule out all types of field work which involve an observer objectifying others for the sake of the former's research. Nor can they privilege the various forms of action research, where the objectives, methods and reporting of the research are all situated within a dialogical relationship between the intellectual and the community for whom the research, allegedly, is designed. This dialogical relationship can be direct, or indirect, as when a researcher is commissioned by a public body of some kind to undertake advocacy-oriented research on behalf of a particular group, for example, menopausal women or homeless teenagers. Evidently, action research does not obviate the problematic of what thereby becomes a professional/client relationship, but a mobilized polity around a particular research project can require of this professional a genuine accountability for their methods of procedure and findings.

It is a good measure of Academe that, when research ethics and methods are taught, it is objective rather than action research that is in question. For good reason, the problematic of the observer is occluded, and students are inducted into the authority of the intellectual. To use Veblen's phrase, they have a trained incapacity in respect of competing and conflicting demands for accountability to different types of audience.

Oppositional Intellectuals and the Non-resolvable Problematic of Their Observer Status

Up until now, oppositional intellectuals have been intellectuals who hold onto their authority as intellectuals, but place it in service to non-dominant groups or classes. They have espoused the old, genteel professional ethic of "service." The democratizing claims of the social movements of the 1960's, 1970's and 1980's have problematized the intellectual's authority as well as that of the professional. In this context, a profession of oppositional values is not sufficient to indicate an intellectual's support for these democratizing claims. What matters is how they practice their authority as an intellectual and whether they open it up to being both problematized and made accountable to different audiences.

Profession of critical values and good intentions, indeed, serves to uphold the intellectual's authority. It reinstates a *communitas* of intellectual virtue shared, at least ideally, by all intellectuals. Within such a community of virtue, differences are rendered a matter of individually professed values and are not allowed to sunder the shared commitments to foundationalist epistemological procedures. Post-foundationalist epistemological procedures deconstruct the transparency of good intentions and the sovereignty of authorship. Thus, when they invite an open contest of differently positioned knowledge claims, they are doing something other than reinventing an intellectual liberalism.

Liberalism always presupposes rational closure of debate, whether the idea of closure is held to be an operational possibility or ideal. A politics of representation is premised on the ideas that not only is there no possibility of resolution of contesting claims, but they are complicit with each other in ways that are not at all transparent in respect of their authors' intentions. The positioning of those who make the claims is a function of this field of discursive contestation. That is, it cannot be declared in advance, but emerges within the perspectively-oriented differences that constitute this field.

It follows that it is important to work to open up the Academy—admission and assessment policies, methods of teaching, academic publishing and means of communication in general—to a politics of representation. In particular, this means doing what is situationally appropriate in order to open up space for non-resolvable dialogues between those who are differently positioned in relation to this politics of representation. It is to develop the polity that any particular and contingently bounded community engaged in a politics of representation comprises.

Once this point is made it necessarily begins to implicate the relationship of intellectuals to those they constitute as non-intellectuals (see Bauman, 1987, ch's. 1 and 2). Oppositional intellectuals, who are willing to work with the problematic of intellectual domination, are likely to see themselves as committed to extending access into the credentialling authority of the academy. They are also likely to be interested in and committed to working with non-intellectuals to develop an experimental practice of partnership in harnessing knowledge to the needs of the polity they together comprise.

In the Australian context, the first of these implicates policy issues which extend access into higher education through a number of means, including effective articulation arrangements with TAFE (Technical and Further Education). Essentially, it is a cluster of practical efforts—which must include practice within the classroom as well as curriculum—to ensure that the credentialling hierarchical levels of the education system are as close to having an open admissions policy as they can be.

The second of these is predicated on a model of differentiated contributions to political practice and struggle. Here the oppositional intellectual has a responsibility which goes beyond working their side of the relationship between theory-based knowledges and practice-based knowledges, as occurs, for example, when intellectuals work with policy-makers, program managers, and professional service-deliverers to apply their (theory-based) knowledge. If policy-makers etc. are, in a real sense, practice-oriented intellectuals, the requirements of their practice environments impose first loyalties to something other than "knowledge." This positions them as those who put the authority of applied knowledge in the service of the state or of a single profession. To the extent that state and professional authority are represented as based in knowledge, the bids for power of intellectuals, policy-makers and professional service-deliverers converge. They all partake of what can be termed professional domination—the determination of the needs of others by those armed with professional knowledge—in relation to those constituted as the objects of professional knowledge (non-professionals). This convergence should not be allowed to occlude the significance of the differences in the ways that they are positioned in relation to the whole world of the generation, transmission and application of professional knowledge.

If what I am terming oppositional intellectuals are so positioned as to be free from having to give their first loyalty to the state or to a *particular* profession (medicine or social work, for example), it is important to understand that many "oppositional" policy-makers and service deliverers depend on the presence of those with this degree of "independence." It is not that the former lack in understanding of the importance of designing policies and services so as to be responsive to the "voice" of non-professionals. Rather, they need the oppositional intellectual to use her freedom to make this understanding explicit.

Two further points need to be made. First, the oppositional intellectual's advocacy on behalf of non-professionals is no advocacy at all if the former adopts an immediate identification with the latter, and refuses thereby to observe them.

Oppositional intellectuals cannot advocate for, in the sense of identifying with, non-professionals without abandoning their deconstructive insights into their own membership of the New Class, where this class's bid for power operates to empower professionals at the expense of non-professionals. What they can do is cooperate with non-professionals who contest professional domination of their needs, and of the services which provide those needs. Such cooperation would mean accepting this contest, and working with its presence within what is constituted as a polity of contested professional domination.

This, then, is a politics of accepting the non-resolvability of what Said termed the problematic of the observer. Where Johannes Fabian, who has contributed an important work in understanding the problematic of observer (Fabian, 1983), seeks to overcome the problematic (Fabian, 1990), post-foundationalist feminist and postcolonial intellectuals can contribute to showing over and over again this non-resolvability and its irrefragable nature.

Second, it is precisely the oppositional intellectual's "observer" status and role which are of value to reflective and critical policy-makers and professional service-deliverers. Intellectually credible "observation" of the lives and needs of non-professionals is central to the business of making reasonably good and democratic policy. In so saying, it is clear that observed needs cannot displace expressed needs. However, observed needs—for example, demographic representation of a particular locality's health needs—provide a comparative context of assessment for expressed needs by showing the comparative status of the locality in relation to others. Does this locality have more or less of a concentration of categories of users who need regular and sometimes intensive health services (e.g. infants, and the frail aged)? Moreover, when the professional observer's mediation of a non-professional's expressed needs operates as in social surveys, interviews and participant observation, this mediation is also designed to comparatively contextualize these needs in relation to the standpoint of either the academic observer and/or the policy-maker. This standpoint permits the emergence of particular *categories* of need. For example, if it turns out that teenage pregnancy or homelessness are socially patterned in ways which put members of particular groups at risk, this kind of observation implicitly constitutes a claim on policy, a claim which policy-makers may take up and make explicit.

Even techniques of observation which permit ethnographic or qualitative representation of non-professionals cannot substitute for their expressed needs. In this connection, the Australian Commonwealth government's sponsorship of needs-based planning in both the child care and home and community care programs of early–mid 1980's offers a useful model for the differentiation and articulation of both the professionals' and non-professionals' respective constructions of need. Needs-based planning was designed to articulate "objective," observer-generated research, mostly of a demographic kind, with direct consultation of those who would be either actual or potential users of the service in question. Thus, for example, aged home care delivery was planned not just in terms of the demographic distribution of need but in relation to the consultation of older people and their carers as to how they saw their needs and how they might best be met. While consultation may take the form of an interview with someone in their own home, it should be regarded as a consultation rather than an interview because of the explicit dialogical nature of the exchange. When the professional consultant approaches a middle-aged Italian woman in one of the inner western suburbs of Adelaide to find out what services she may need to assist her as the carer of her severely demented, incontinent mother-in-law, this becomes an exchange because not only does the professional have to make her approach in Italian but to delicately engage this carer in judging her own needs and how they best be met. Delicacy is needed especially because it is not culturally legitimate for this carer to directly express difficulty or resentment in relation to the stress she bears in looking after her mother-in-law.

When expressed needs are worked into the design of a service or program, the conditions for a polity of exchange and dialogue between the professionals and non-professionals involved are operative. Other conditions are needed for this polity to develop, but the point to emphasize here is that this relationship, no more than the more one-sided observation-directed relationships, does not equalize the position of the two parties to the relationship. Their position remains both different and incommensurable.

Concluding Remarks

Foundationalist epistemologies de-problematize and naturalize the knowing subject-object relationship by making epistemological procedures appear in line with the nature of things. They thereby de-politicize this relationship, and the most they may require of an epistemological politics is a confession of values on the part of the sovereign author, which once made is safely sequestered from science. Foundationalist epistemologies actively legitimize the bid for power of the New Class, and deeply implicate it in the modern, Western, state-centric, imperialist and capitalist system of domination.

At a time of unparalleled assertion of difference, foundationalist social science is regrouping so as to accommodate difference within the politics of vertical integration. It does this by revamping liberal pluralism, the methodological individualist equivalent of which is the rational actor's preferences. As is well known, pluralism occludes not only inequality—some are more plural (equal) than others—but also that such inequality is a function of interconnected relationships of domination. Pluralism renders the contemporary politics of difference into a level playing field of special interest groups, and uses market appeal as the central criterion of whether a group has sufficient presence or power to be accorded existence.

Revamped pluralism indicates, in fact, that the project of foundationalist social science is complete: all that can be done under the pressure of contemporary political demands is put new wine in old bottles. What this declares is the irreconcilability of foundationalist epistemologies with a politics of difference, a proposition that makes good logical, even tautological, sense.

Thus, contemporary foundationalist social science has two options whereby to theoretically orient itself: a. to enter into a classicism in respect of its founding texts, with such acknowledgment as is made of the possibility of their anachronism in respect of contemporary politics drowned out by a deferential conversion of them into the origins or foundations of the discipline; b. to acknowledge difference but quickly convert it to become the formal difference of individualized preferences, the subject of neo-classical ("modern") economics, and generalizing the model of *homo economicus* to the whole realm of social action. Neither of these options excludes the other. Both maintain the liberal fiction of the sovereign subject/author, where the idea that there is an origin of knowledge logically maintains the idea of a foundation for knowledge (see Ryan, 1989). Moreover, both declare that the project of modern social science is a completed one. It is thus doomed to repetition and to endless technical refinement.

Postfoundationalist social science confronts the challenges that I have identified. It also confronts those who come to it as intellectuals trained in the modern disciplines of social science with what appear at first as formidable requirements of new learning. Significantly, these demand full immersion in what can be regarded only as an extraordinary wealth of new social and political theorizing, coming, of course, from non-disciplinary directions.

3

The Place of Women's Studies in the Contemporary University

The place of Women's Studies in the contemporary university has to do with making institutionalized knowledge accountable and responsive to contemporary politico-ethical challenges. This role of Women's Studies is one of developing the university in line with contemporary visions and standards of justice. This may seem to make Women's Studies relevant only to the "soft" disciplines of the Humanities and Social Sciences, disciplines that are given explicit permission within the intellectual division of labor to be concerned with "values" and value debate. Of course this is not so. Women's Studies is the site of a radical critique of modern western epistemology. This critique demonstrates the very conception of modern science to depend on a patriarchally invested privilege as the universal knower able to objectify all that becomes his to know. This privilege by its nature excludes women, and all those who fall within the objectified rather than subjectified side of this scientific relationship. Thus, in interrogating their exclusion from modern western knowledge, feminist intellectuals perforce engage in a radical epistemological enterprise which has both deconstructive force and reconstructive potential.

I make these points only to establish that the intellectual enterprise which Women's Studies represents concerns the heartlands of modern science, not simply its "softer," more discursive aspects. The epistemological contribution of Women's Studies is to insist on examining the politics of knowledge production, to enquire into the "who is producing for whom" as well as into the conditions which permit them more-or-less acknowledged authority as knowledge producers.

This epistemological orientation places Women's Studies in a directly contestatory relationship to all academic disciplinary practices which rely for their intellectual authority on the fiction that their substance and method reflect rather than create truth. It is clear, is it not, that if an academic expert claims his knowledge reflects rather than constitutes reality, and if we accept the validity of such a claim, our critical scrutiny concerns only the adequacy of his method or procedure. We do not subject to critical scrutiny his basic assumption that there is one reality in relation to which, in principle at least, rational consensus is possible. Women's Studies, in demonstrating the patriarchal investment in this kind of monorational universalism, *and* its exclusion of all those who are not accepted within the club of rational patriarchs, questions this fundamental assumption as to one reality and indicates an alternative conception of knowledge.

Women's Studies is thus participating at the cutting edge of contemporary critical theory. It has become a formidable protagonist in a theoretically sophisticated politics of knowledge. I will say more of this in what follows, but it is important to acknowledge that most of the contemporary university still manages to insulate itself against the challenges feminism represents. As much as it provides a genuine space for the development of feminist intellectual work, the way in which Women's Studies is institutionalized ensures that it is sequestered and ghettoized in relation to what is regarded as the mainstream aspects of the university. It seems to be a rule that, if women demand space in which to find their own voice, and are successful in indicating the normal rule of masculinized authority does not apply to this space, men tend to evacuate this territory altogether. In leaving Women's Studies to the women, they reinstitute the normal patriarchal gender order of according the highest value to men's business. Among other things, this shelters the university from the renewal of the spirit of rational enquiry that Women's Studies potentially offers. This may be rather dangerous at this point of time when all governments seem intent on using the principles of managerialism to erode, if not destroy, the authority of professional knowledge.

Women's Studies often contributes to its own ghettoization by adopting an insular and even separatist attitude to its intellectual enterprise, while simultaneously depending upon the very mainstream values and practices of the university it lambastes as patriarchal. In this respect, Women's Studies offers nothing to the renewal and rethinking of the idea of the university in the context of government erosion of professional authority and university autonomy. This is a loss which needs redressing. It is the non-traditional parts of the university which can contribute to the rethinking and renewal of the idea of the university in ways that must command the respect of governments precisely because they respond to contemporary criteria of justice and equity.

Unfortunately, most of the academic leadership of the contemporary university is virtual putty in the government's hands. The government is mixing the principles of managerialism and plebiscitary democracy in its efforts to uproot the culture and procedures of academic collegial governance. Inevitably, an academic leadership looking to the past for its erstwhile unquestioned scientific or scholarly authority is poorly placed to defend itself against this agenda. It is especially so when this leadership is sympathetic to the claims on justice in the university by marginalized groups such as women and Maori. To the extent that this leadership sequesters these claims and avoids the painful struggle of entering into a genuine, intellectually-oriented dialogue and debate in relation to them, its conception of the culture of rational enquiry remains backward-looking and defensive, without vision. This also means that the advocates of the new claims on justice are left relatively sheltered from the critical, tough-minded intellectual scrutiny their claims deserve to enjoy if they are to become just claims grounded in a rationally oriented civic culture. This provides a virtual vacuum within which the anti-academic requirements of governments for information rather than knowledge can make themselves felt.

Perhaps the first step in the direction of institutional renewal of rational enquiry occurs when a university is willing to take Women's Studies seriously by demanding of it that it become a genuine academic enterprise with the usual emphases on research-led teaching and a healthy graduate program. This, of course, means that the university is willing to resource this enterprise at the levels which permit it to be research-led. The University of Waikato may be said to have taken this step in its decisions to create a Centre for Women's Studies in 1986, to establish a Foundation Chair of Women's Studies in 1990 (I took up the appointment April 1991), and to give full academic status to Women's Studies by according it departmental status as of January 1, 1993. It is important to see these decisions against the background of longstanding and wide-based efforts of women at this University to develop and, by their own efforts, resource Women's Studies. In 1974 the first two courses were offered in Women's Studies at the University of Waikato: the Sociology of Women by Rosemary Seymour, and Women and Psychology by Sarah Calvert, a graduate student whose capacity to do this was enabled by one of the male academics in Psychology lending his convenorship to the course. Jane Ritchie took over the teaching of Women and Psychology in 1976, and was the Foundation Director of the Centre for Women's Studies. The efforts of all these women alongside the vision of the University's most recent Vice Chancellor has assured the University of Waikato the most established and academically developed program of Women's Studies in New Zealand.

The University of Waikato, by its commitment to biculturalism and to women, breaks with the traditional cultures of universities, and signals its capacity to offer leadership in what are times of considerable challenge to modern Western ideals and values. In offering this leadership, the University of Waikato is showing the distinctive value of university leadership in responding to the challenges of the present time. This value resides in the insistence of the university on both a critically reflective relationship to values and the importance of ensuring that such claims as we want to make about reality are tested by skepticism as to both their empirical and their theoretical validity.

Perhaps never more than at this time is the idea of the university so important. For it is in these times that the whole tradition of Western culture and knowledge has come under challenge from those whom it has marginalized, those whom the West has colonized, and those whom it has treated as secondary to the main business at hand. One of these groups, of course, is women. The temptation, in the context of these challenges to the whole authority of the Western knowledge, has been to throw the baby out with the bath water. This is a challenge we should resist. Let me give an example of the kinds of challenges that I think we are experiencing at the present, and of how they affect the development of Women's Studies. Women's Studies came into being with the development of the second wave of the feminist movement toward the end of the 1960's, at a time in which a higher education system, a university system, was well established in advanced capitalist countries. By this time it was a mass university system in the United States, and at the point at which Women's Studies became institutionalized as a part of the curricula in the 1980's, this quality of being a mass system had extended to Australian and New Zealand higher education as well.

The social movements of the sixties drew much of their base from university students and it was inevitable that the kinds of claims they were making, both in terms of values and in terms of claims about the nature of reality, would find reflection in academic curriculum. So the second wave of the feminist movement was taken up within the university and expressed as Women's Studies. This means that Women's Studies is necessarily bound up with the projects of professionalization that the contemporary university represents. The first wave of feminism, the wave that we associate with the second half of the nineteenth century and the first two decades of this century, was coterminous with the professionalization of knowledge. Not only was there an especial attraction for nineteenth century feminists of the professional ideals of career open to talent and of trained service, but many of these feminist reformers were profoundly engaged with projects that laid the groundwork for social work and the other human services as professions.[1] The confluence of the first wave of feminism with that of professionalization did not mean that feminist values were allowed to contaminate the culture of scientific objectivity and value-neutrality which characterized the ethos of the professions. That now there is an open politics of contesting and contestable knowledge claims within the contemporary university is an important change which may owe more to the subjection of the university to "outside" political influence than to the self-regulation of the collegial community of the autonomous university.[2] Such political influence represents a demand that the public universities democratize themselves, in the sense of being more accountable to the community of tax-paying citizens which funds them. Such democratization has been understood to mean that universities should adapt their entry and other credentialling procedures so as to permit access and entry to groups traditionally poorly represented in higher education. It has been also understood to mean that the values of movements placed in a contestatory relationship to modern Western, patriarchal rationalism should enter the intellectual debates of the university.

This politicization of the university has been understood by many of the custodians of Western, masculinist reason to constitute a threat to the very foundations of the university. There is an uneasy and often highly conflictual relationship between the older principle of rational enquiry and that of multiple, contestable and openly politicized claims on "truth." Where this relationship works as a binary opposition between two camps in the contemporary university, there is a dreadful game played out between a scientistic representation of rational enquiry, on the one hand, and "politically correct" forms of moral certitude on the other. Necessarily, the first wins hands down since the latter abandons all pretense to rational enquiry and commits itself to moral terror as its practice. The promise for the future lies in refusing this binarism and in an open, reflective embrace of the tensions which arise as to the question of what rational enquiry means in a universe of multiple, politicized truth claims where there can be no monorational mode of closure for debate. The politics of Women's Studies within the contemporary university is thoroughly subject to the tensions between rational enquiry and political correctness. However, it is arguable that it has been assisted in making this a productive and creative intellectual enterprise by a further development, the challenge to Western (white and middle class) feminism by non-Western women and women of color. This challenge has unsettled the moral certainties of this movement-oriented intellectual discipline and propelled it into its own distinctive sociology of knowledge.

The feminist movement has been increasingly challenged, from about the end of the 1970's onward, by non-Western women and by women of color. These challenges have brought out the neglect of class, racist, and ethnic oppression by the feminist movement, with its tendency to concentrate on gender issues. Those making these challenges have said over and over again that the feminist movement's tendency to oppose women to men overlooks the critical fact that, for black women, depending on the context, racist oppression may be often more primary than gender oppression, and that in opposing racism their allies are black men, not white women. This kind of politics is expressed by the Afro-American feminist theorist bell hooks (1984,1–2) who declares:

> Feminism in the United States has never emerged from the women who are most victimized by sexist oppression: women who are daily beaten down, mentally, physically and spiritually, women who are powerless to change their condition in life. They are a silent majority. A mark of their victimization is that they accept their lot in life without visible question, without organized protest, without collective anger or rage. Betty Friedan's *The Feminine Mystique* is still heralded as having paved the way for the contemporary feminist movement—it was written as if these women did not exist. Friedan's famous phrase, "the problem that has no name," often quoted to describe the condition of women in this society, actually referred to the plight of a select group of college-educated, middle and upper class, married white women—housewives bored with leisure, with the home, with children, with buying products, who wanted more out of life....She did not discuss who would be called in to take care of the children and maintain the home, if more women like herself were freed from their house labor and given equal access with white men to the professions.

bell hooks (1984,18) also makes the point that the feminist ideal of equality with men tacitly presupposes shared class, race and ethnic group status with dominant group men. It does not make sense for women who are racially, economically, ethnically exploited to seek equality with their male peers:

> Knowing that men in their groups do not have social, political and economic power, they could not deem it liberatory to share their social status. While they are aware that sexism enables men in their respective groups to have privileges denied them, they are more likely to see exaggerated expressions of male chauvinism among their peers as stemming from the male's sense of himself as powerless and ineffectual in relation to ruling male groups rather than an expression of an overall privileged social status.

It is logical that the only women who are positioned to make gender inequality their primary concern are those of dominant race, ethnic and class status. However, this is not an insight achieved by these women on their own: it has depended on challenges from women positioned in ways which exclude them from this privilege. The effect of these challenges has been to make evident the interested quality of feminist politics and ideology, an interestedness that expresses the tendency of its leaders and followers to be white, western and middle-class. Thus Nancy Cott (1987, 9), a feminist historiographer of US feminism, makes this quite clear in the introduction to *The Grounding of Modern Feminism*: "The woman's rights tradition was historically initiated by, and remains prejudiced toward, those who perceive themselves first and foremost as 'woman', who can gloss over their class, racial, and other status identifications because those are culturally dominant and therefore relatively invisible."

If this is generally true of feminism, it is especially true of its professional domains: femocracy (see Yeatman, 1990b, chapters four and five; and Sawer, 1990) and Women's Studies. The degree to which academic practitioners of Women's Studies have been willing to respond to these challenges has been mixed. It is fair to say that the theoretical work with which Women's Studies is currently associated is a genuine and positive response to those challenges. There are several aspects of this response. First, there is a deconstructive response, which demonstrates that feminism as critique necessarily confirms the very ground it seeks to challenge. Thus feminism as critique tends to reproduce and confirm the binarisms of a patriarchal gender division of labor, and, paradoxically, becomes complicit with that order.[3] This deconstructive response conduces to an examination of the history of how Women's Studies and feminism have participated in western, white and masculinist modes of knowledge. For example, there is work on how white women in colonial settings were and are complicit in a gendered way with white, western, masculinist colonization, and on how this colonization has inscribed the policing binarism of "good" and "bad" women within the racialized hierarchies of colonizer and colonized (see Haggis, 1990; Haggis, 1992; and Jolly, 1993).

A second response to these challenges has been a theory of the intersections between different bases of oppression, that is, working with the idea that there are multiple bases of oppression, that there is class, gender, ethnicity, race, sexuality, and that not any one of these bases of oppression can be viewed as a master key to the rest, that they have to be treated analytically separately and then examined in their historically specific intersections. This is making for some mature and exciting work (see Bottomley et al., 1991; and Stasiulis,1990).

A third response which is clearly indicated by the second is the opening up in theoretical and practical terms of a politics of voice and representation within Women's Studies. Specifically, in theoretical terms, Women's Studies is beginning to debate the proposition that white western women cannot speak for all women. It is now accepted that for all women to be a part of Women's Studies a dialogical process has to be opened up which is open to differently positioned women, that is, women who regard themselves as differently positioned in terms of ethnicity, race, class and sexuality. This is a politics of difference and it is arguable that it is predicated on abandoning a radical feminist insistence on the unity of women. This is a highly contentious proposition at the current time, especially as it calls into question ideas of immediate and transparent personal experience and face-to-face community. Iris Young (1990a) argues against the totalizing tendency of these ideas and the way in which they work to suppress or to deny difference, and she is one of the more significant feminist theorists of a democratic politics of difference.[4]

These theoretical responses are emergent, they have a kind of maturity, but they have a long way to go. They are participating in a more general theoretical renaissance. Women's Studies, or, more adequately, the feminist theory that I have indicated, is contributing to a significant new wave of theorizing in the humanities and the social sciences, a wave just as significant as the intellectual revolution which psychoanalysis, sociology and anthropology brought about at the turn of the nineteenth century into the twentieth century. This new body of theory is both supremely skeptical and democratic in relation to the values which are always embedded in knowledge. It refuses to authorize any knowledge claim that makes that claim appear as though it is grounded in the nature of things, as though it is a mirror image of something out there that is simply true. This is a radical skepticism which accepts Nietzsche's proposition that truths are metaphors. This is because truths are a function of the politics of representation, it being representations rather than reflections of reality that are at issue. My point is that such skepticism is in the traditions of the modern university. It is democratic because it is able to use methods of analysis which show how any positive representation of humanity tends to "other" that which it is not. This kind of analysis creates a space for those who have been "othered" in discourse.

Feminist representations construct their own representational economies of inclusions and exclusions. An example of this is the commonly held feminist view that women are more cooperative than men. The new critical theorizing problematizes all aspects of that statement. It questions for whom and in what contexts it is meaningful to speak of all women. Secondly, it suggests that, if some insist on speaking for all women, this is because they are naturalizing the condition of being a woman, a rhetorical gambit that contradicts precisely where feminist interventions tend to operate, namely to denaturalize, to refuse to essentialize this business of being a woman. It also brings out the way in which the proposition that women are more cooperative than men necessarily conforms to a binary politics of inversion which "others" men, and conflates who men might become with a patriarchal, masculinist *status quo*. This particular representation also "others" women who are not cooperative or who refuse to conform to what cooperative means within the rhetorical context at hand.

If the new critical theorizing problematizes this kind of binary categorical claim for women it does so in a spirit of self-critical irony. It accepts not only as a condition of feminism that such binary categorizing is necessary. It makes it clear that the very necessity of feminism arises from the material existence of a patriarchal ideological binary and hierarchical ordering of the terms male (masculine, men) and female (feminine, women). In short, this theorizing adopts a deconstructive relationship to its own discursive practice (see especially Riley, 1988; and Butler, 1990).

This example underlines the point that feminist theory has matured to the point where it is able to subject its own premises to an ironical, skeptical and critical mode of analysis. Here I join and celebrate with Teresa de Lauretis (1988, 138–139) in her statement that:

> A feminist theory begins when the feminist critique of ideologies becomes conscious of itself, and turns to question its own body of writing and critical interpretations, its basic assumptions and terms and the practices which they enable and from which they emerge. This is not merely an expansion or a reconfiguration of boundaries, but a qualitative shift in political and historical consciousness. This shift implies, in my opinion, a dis-placement and a self-displacement: leaving or giving up a place that is safe, that is "home,"(physically, emotionally, linguistically and epistemologically) for another place that is unknown and risky, that is not only emotionally but conceptually other, a place of discourse from which speaking and thinking are at best tentative, uncertain and unguaranteed. But the leaving is not a choice: one could not live there in the first place.

De Lauretis (1988, 139) goes on to say: "Both dis-placements, the personal and the conceptual, are painful—either the cause or the result of the pain, risk and a real stake." This thematic of how an open politics of representation, tied as it is into a contemporary politics of difference, requires us to relinquish that great icon of the cult of domesticity—"home" as refuge and sanctuary in relation to the fray of the public marketplace—is importantly developed by Minnie Bruce Pratt in her "Identity: Skin Blood Heart." There Pratt, a white, middle class, Protestant, Southern US woman, shows how the home of her childhood was predicated on strictly and violently policed exclusion of all that is (who are) not white, middle class, Protestant, "normal," thus prescribing her own exclusion as the lesbian she becomes later.[5]

I offer this quick sketch, and that is all it is, of how contemporary, critical, feminist theorizing operates, to indicate how far it is from ideological self-congratulation and dogma, and how much it participates in the critical, reflective and skeptical spirit of a university. My argument is also that it is this spirit which is as central now as it ever was to a democratic and non-totalizing politics. It is undoubtedly true that such critical theorizing depends on the legitimacy a university affords not only to critical reflection but to the erudition and scholarship on which such reflection depends. In short, the professionalism of modern university-based knowledge is required for this critical theorizing to be possible.

If, then, we acknowledge the merit of the by-now established lines of critique of professional domination, it cannot be because those of us who are critical feminist theorists are willing to abandon our professionalism. It is arguable that all professions make a bid for power through their monopoly on particular kinds of knowledge claim. It is this which is at issue in the critiques of professional domination, as with the women's health movement in relation to the medical profession. It is no less at issue in respect of critical feminist theorists. The fact that this is so, however, does not warrant the abolition of the authority which resides in scholarly erudition and expertise. The answer lies not in attempting to preempt the differentiation of expert and non-expert feminist theorizing by making all conform to the homogenizing dictates of feminist community and its inevitable, totalizing moral strictures. Instead, it lies in maintaining this differentiation while requiring both dialogue and accountability across it.

Just what this might mean requires rather different models of political accountability, dialogue and democratic participation than those we inherit. I was permitted some insight into these models by a consultancy I did, an evaluation of the largest home and community care service type in South Australia. This evaluation was jointly sponsored by the Commonwealth and South Australian Governments. Its context was both fraught and complex: the stakeholders comprised the bureaucrats of both governments (these manifested inter- and intra-agency tensions), the managers of the services concerned, the direct service deliverers (allied health professionals and paramedical aides, almost all women), the consumers and carers, plus a range of interested third parties (local government, older people's advocacy groups and so on). The strain of increasingly rationed and scarce services was most acutely felt by the direct service deliverers, consumers and carers. The latter were angry not only about the lack of service but its delivery in ways that did not always respect the expressed needs of consumers and carers.

One of the most important lines of conflict concerned precisely the ethos of professional domination which colored the service. On the service-delivery side, commitment to this ethos was much more strongly maintained by the medical directors of each regional service than by the allied health professionals. Most of the paramedical aides had been recruited from enrolled nurses, and had been trained in a culture of professional domination. Doctors tend to be quite sure not only that they can discern the "real" needs of the patient but that these needs are more real than the expressed needs of the patient—in short, that they know the needs of patients better than patients know their own needs, and that, therefore, the voice of a patient is a redundancy in his or her receiving a service. The disabled consumers in this service area tend to be veterans of the disability movement, a movement oriented in part to contesting precisely this professional paternalism in service delivery. So, there was eloquent and sustained protest against the ethos of professional domination from the most active consumers. They were supported in this by the Commonwealth Government's declared commitment to designing services around the need of individuals rather than *vice versa*. The doctors interpreted this debate as a zero-sum game: either they continued to be God, or civilization (science) as we have known it would disappear. The consumers were more sophisticated. If one listened closely, and picked one's way through their rhetoric of frustration and anger at not being heeded by the service, they were suggesting there is a place for both expert-defined *and* expressed needs, and that the issue was one of ensuring an effective and reciprocally accountable relationship between these two types of need, and the actors voicing them. Since I had no doubt that expert knowledge and professional experience were crucial to the quality of the service, and I rightly discerned an anti-professionalism in the bureaucrats' brief with which I wished to be non-complicit, I worked on a partnership model of a dialogical relationship between the service deliverers on the one hand, and the consumers and carers on the other.

This model democratizes the service-delivery relationship but does so in a way which does not homogenize the roles of all the parties to that relationship. Each becomes the appropriate "expert" for their distinctive role. Since the parties are non-substitutable in the relationship, the voice of each must contribute to the working and development of that relationship. There is a strong likelihood of differences in judgement and policy for the relationship arising. Some of these may be irresolvable. This notwithstanding, the partnership model requires the differentiated parties to the relationship to be dialogically accountable to each other for these differences and to be responsible for negotiated pragmatic compromises which permit, if not consensus, a decision with which all can live for the time being. For such a partnership to be possible, the parties concerned have to be resourced. Professionals have to be trained to be accountable in these ways and consumers need to know that there are information and advocacy services they can call on if they need them. This partnership model actually privileges all the parties. It does not invert the usual relationship of professional domination by making the consumer, rather than the professional, top dog. Indeed, we should be wary of contemporary governmental policy which is making the consumer sovereign. By a relative marginalization of professional knowledge (and a relative deprofessionalization of human services), governments are achieving a cheapening of services but are depriving consumers and carers of the contribution of expert knowledge to the process of defining and meeting their needs.

The partnership model solves some of the problems we have inherited from the democratic tradition. The alternative to representative models of democracy has been participatory democracy, which has been understood in terms of face-to-face community and a politics of equality. Everyone is put on the same level, difference is not able to be worked with, and, inevitably, those most adept at manipulating the communitarian ethos of the interaction prevail.

How far is this model of a democratized, expert-informed service delivery relevant to working out the relationship of university-based Women's Studies to women and the women's movement outside the university? Should the academic enterprise of Women's Studies be understood as analogous to the delivery of a service, and, if so, to whom is this service delivered?

The fundamental obligation of a university-based Women's Studies practitioner is to be an expert in terms of the conventions of scholarly expertise which characterize the contemporary university. In this regard, her service delivery roles concern her university-based constituencies: primarily her students, both undergraduate and graduate, whom she is inducting into this scholarly discipline, but also her academic peers, and the academic management of the institution to whom she is responsible for her university practice. For her *expertise*, accountability to these constituencies overrides accountability to extra-university constituencies.

Academics in the politically marked university disciplines—such as Women's Studies and Maori Studies—are accountable also to extra-university constituencies of those who make claims on them through shared political and movement affiliation. For her politics, accountability to these constituencies overrides accountability to the university-based constituencies. However, as will be clear, this is not a simple issue.

If the Women's Studies academic has an obligation of accountability for her value orientation and her politics to these constituencies, on the model of partnership I have offered above this obligation cannot be understood as one which requires her to deny the ways in which her scholarly expertise informs her values and politics.[6] These ways make her a critical and reflective participant in politically-oriented dialogue, and she may often substitute reflection for policy action to the justifiable frustration of those oriented to action. In this context, she has a dual obligation: 1. to be an effective communicator in relation to these non-academic constituencies; 2. to appreciate and respect their expressed needs for how she realizes her role in relation to them, which, among other things, may require that she become more familiar with the world of policy action.

The requirement of effective communication requires her to become bi- if not multi-lingual in the sense of being able to operate across different contextually bound dialects and modes of rhetoric. Anyone who aspires to be a public intellectual must develop these lingual competences. Her own academic language must appear as so much arcane jargon to non-initiates. Lingual difference of this kind is one of the clear hallmarks of the line dividing expert from non-expert knowledge. Her academic language is appropriate for the university classroom and for communication to her academic peers. It is not appropriate for communication to non-academic audiences, but, again, her "plain" language competences will be always colored by the byzantine intricacies and esoterica of her academic tongue. What her "mother" tongue is, is a moot point since like all intellectuals her self(ves) has(ve) become re-created through the rhetorical artifice of the modern intellectual disciplines.

It cannot be denied that those who claim expertise have a tendency to construe their relationship to the non-expert along hierarchical lines so that the former believe they know *in general* more than the latter, that their esoteric language makes them *in general* cleverer and more insightful than the latter. These beliefs are clearly undemocratic. If, ultimately, knowledge is oriented by some reference to need, it is clear that no amount of expert attention to need can substitute for what I have called above "expressed" need, or need as constructed by those who have the need. The non-expert knowledge of needy persons is just as much crafted by experience and learning as is expert knowledge. They remain, however, different kinds of knowledge.

Much of my argument here concerns this difference and its importance. If it is important to require Women's Studies academics to be politically accountable to the expressed needs of women's movement constituencies, it is equally important to accept that their expert knowledge has a place in relation to these expressed needs. This kind of knowledge permits these needs to be historically situated, critically and reflectively analyzed. Among other things, this ensures that the interested quality of feminism, its inflection by the privileged race, ethnic and class positioning of its follower, is subject to critical challenge and reflection. This, in turn, conduces to a democratic politics of difference within feminism, one in which it is accepted that the needs of differently positioned women are different. The values of reflective critique, empirically oriented enquiry and logically coherent analysis remain as crucial to the health of an emancipatory social movement such as the women's movement as they are in general to a society oriented within democratic, dialogical and civil process.

Part Two

Refiguring the Polity

4

Beyond Natural Right
The Conditions for Universal Citizenship

Introduction

Postcolonial conditions, the success of the welfare state in delegitimizing old ideas of hierarchy based in class or race, and the contemporary feminist movement all have had the effect of forcing us to think again about what we mean by "citizenship" and what it might take to establish equality within any particular community of citizens. Here I want to argue that the dominant framework through which we have approached questions of citizenship in the modern epoch is manifestly inadequate in the face of these challenges. This dominant framework is based on the tradition of natural right and on the particular ideas of individual freedom which that tradition involves.

There have been important and powerful challenges to this dominant tradition. Here I want to consider two alternative accounts of modern citizenship. The first locates citizenship claims in membership of a complex system of interdependencies based in an advanced division of labor. If one can claim to be fulfilling a specialized role within this system one can claim citizenship. This is a corporative view of citizenship, advanced by Durkheim and other late nineteenth and early twentieth century "progressives." It also had strong resonance in the argument of "first-wave" feminists that women's citizenship claim was proper and just because it reflected their distinctive, specialized societal role: maternal nurturance and its domestic and extra-domestic expressions.

The second alternative account of modern citizenship is based on the proposition that natural right necessarily privileges those most favored by "nature," prior to any positive social intervention. In order to create a basis for equality of citizenship, this account argues that the state must establish "social" rights for all. The state must become a welfare state, and provide a set of institutional entitlements to services which allow all to enjoy a basic standard of life, without which political and civil rights are meaningless. Here individuality or individual freedom is made contingent on access to socially provided rights.

These two alternative accounts of citizenship do not actually supplant the one based in the tradition of natural right. Instead, they modify and complement it. In this sense the tradition of natural right remains the dominant account, which is one important reason why there has been a renaissance of pure, unmodified natural right theory in the small-government/minimal-state politics of the present time. In order for there to be a genuine alternative to natural right theories of citizenship, we need an alternative understanding of individuality, and, thus, of the freedom through which it can be expressed. In the final section of this paper, I briefly examine indications that such an alternative understanding is emerging.

Citizenship becomes a paramount value when the modern conception of action is elaborated into a world view. In this world view the existence and reproduction of social life is understood as dependent on human action and its historical dynamics. It is because humans are attributed the freedom to make themselves and the world they live in that citizenship becomes necessary. To be a citizen is to be accorded both rights of membership of a particular self-determining community of action, and respect by that community for one's own freedom to be a self-determining actor. Citizenship then articulates the conditions of freedom of action where these concern two mutually dependent spheres of action: 1. the macro sphere of action which entails a self-determining (self-governing) community, or political society; and 2. the micro sphere of action, which entails the freedom of action of individual members of the political society as this is upheld by the institutions and culture of this society. In other words, it does not make sense to accord individuals rights as individual actors without simultaneously constituting them as a community that will uphold these rights and that, in order to do so, must itself be self-determining.

There is then a reciprocal relationship between the citizen community and the individual citizen's rights. The latter can be upheld and developed only as they are guaranteed by the culture and institutions of the citizen community; and these institutions and cultures can be upheld and developed only as individual citizens require them to be. It follows that individuals cannot expect to have real as opposed to ideal rights if they are not committed to working on behalf of the self-determination of the whole political community. Nor, of course, can the whole of this political community expect this commitment to be forthcoming unless it is pursuing policies and programs which actively foster individual capacities and freedom of action.

The mutual dependence of these macro (communal) and micro (individual) levels of the self-determining properties of action is obvious once stated. We need to establish why the obviousness of this point becomes lost in the tradition of natural right, and how the obscuring of this point makes this tradition a fundamentally problematic and primitive approach to the requirements of modern citizenship.

Natural Right Theories of Action

Historically, the first elaborations of the idea of freedom of action took the form of theories of natural right. Theorists such as Grotius, Hobbes, Locke, and Rousseau were central architects of this conception of action in terms of natural right. The basic features of this conception appear in these statements by Grotius (Tuck, 1979, 70, 73):

> Things belonging to individuals are by nature inalienable or alienable.
>
> Inalienable things are things which belong so essentially to one man that they could not belong to another, as a man's life, body, freedom, honor.
>
> Right Reason and the Nature of Society...does not prohibit all Manner of Violence, but only that which is repugnant to Society, that is, which invades another's Right: For the Design of Society is, that everyone should quietly enjoy his own, with the Help and by the united Force of the whole Community.

Freedom to be an actor then is understood as freedom to be one's own agent, as freedom to control one's own, and as freedom from interference with such control by others.

The significance of basing this freedom in "natural" right is twofold. First, it makes this right prior and absolute with regard to existing social claims and obligations. If these do not accord with the requirements of natural right they are rendered illegitimate contraventions of nature. Second, an appeal to "nature" as a base for legitimation indicates that, at the outset, the modern culture of action could stake its claims only through dispute as to how the divinely created constitution of human nature and its external environment required human nature to be expressed.

In short, modern exponents of action were forced to appeal to a traditional religious frame of reference in order to develop this profoundly nontraditional and secular value: action. Theirs was a profoundly paradoxical position: God creates humans and their world, but God requires of humans that they become the agents of their own, "worldly" fate and that they make active use of their environment for their own use and convenience. This is a God who requires of his human creation a rational and industrious agency, where as Locke (1965, 293) put it, "Action" becomes "the great business of Mankind." Indeed, Locke's god requires his human actors to "subdue" the earth and to improve "the Arts and Sciences and the conveniences of Life."[1]

Natural right, then, began with a traditional starting point—divinely created nature—in order to emancipate individuals as actors in relation to the traditionally legitimated authorities of absolute monarchy, scholasticism, the church, and kinship. The force of this argument of emancipation was immediate and radical.

For God creates human beings as actors, beings who can govern and direct themselves by means of the faculty of reason with which God has endowed them. Insofar as individuals submit to the law of reason they are capable of self-government (Locke 1965, 347–348, par. 57). They can become their own authorities in matters of intellectual, moral, and political concern. Accordingly, it is up to them to choose what occupation they follow, whom they will marry, which system of philosophy they find persuasive, and who will be their political representatives and governors.

This claim to self-government fundamentally eroded the legitimacy of the various traditional forms of patrimonial government, in which authority is based in the idea of a naturally based hierarchy of superordination and subordination, and in which rights of superordination derive either from patriarchal, kin-based authority or from a divinely conferred title to rule. A patrimonial culture, indeed, is one oriented to the legitimacy of tradition, where what counts is the renewal of divinely authorized ways of seeing and doing, and where action is denied legitimacy. Within a patrimonial culture individuals cannot legitimately be their own agents, and the value of self-determination at either the micro or macro level cannot find anchorage in this type of culture.

The emancipation of the individual's freedom of action is what constitutes individuality, namely the freedom and capacity to act. To be an individual is the same as to be an actor.[2] The emancipation of the individual is simultaneously the emancipation of the community. If individuals become free to act, then structures of authority which constitute the government of this community must respect individual agency. This means that all authority binding individuals is legitimate only if it is mediated by their rational agency. Individuals must rationally judge the expressions of authority and make that judgement the arbiter of the acceptability of those expressions. The upshot of this is to require some form of democratic government of the community to which these individuals belong. Moreover, this government must respect not only the capacity for self-government of individuals but express this capacity on behalf of all taken as a community. Action, in short, cannot become the frame of reference for individuals without simultaneously becoming the frame of reference for the communities they comprise.

The traditional starting point of natural right theory also makes the relationship between individual actors and the agentic community they comprise fundamentally problematic. Individuals are accorded a natural standing, and the agentic community they comprise is accorded a secondary and artificial standing. This is because the agentic community is viewed as the outcome and expression of human action, whereas human actors themselves are conceived as divinely created. The actors enjoy a privilege of origins that the agentic community does not, and the result is to privilege the "individual" in relation to "society."

This logic draws even more force from how the traditional starting point of natural right theories is elaborated. Paradoxically, again, the assertion of the individual's freedom to act is made in the form of a democratization of patrimonial authority. That is, one becomes an individual if one is one's own lord or master, with jurisdiction over one's own particular *dominium*.

Thus, when the first natural right theories proposed that all men are born free, they took this to mean that men are not born subject to the lordship of another. Locke is particularly clear on this point. He speaks (1965, 346, par. 54) of "the Equality which all Men are in, in respect of Jurisdiction or Dominion one over another," and of "that equal Right that every Man hath, to his Natural Freedom, without being subjected to the will or authority of any other Man." It followed as Rousseau (1968, 7) argues: "Since no man has a natural authority over his fellow, and force creates no right, we must conclude that conventions form the basis of all legitimate authority among men."

A field for action was opened up, then, by democratizing and individualizing the patrimonial idea of dominion. To be sure, the individualization of dominion turned it into the modern idea of private property. The administrative-territorial-governmental connotations of the idea of domination were transmuted as this idea was turned into the notion of private control and mastery by an individual agent or subject over an object domain. At the same time, the origins of the individual's freedom of action in the idea of patrimonial dominion left a mark on how this freedom was conceived and on the kind of individuality it required. To be an individual requires that one be lord and master over one's own domestic domain, one's own household. As we shall see this means that not all persons could be "individuals." Inevitably, the political government, which has to be structured so as to recognize the patrimonial dominion of all the individuals who accept its jurisdiction, appears as less rooted in the nature of reality than the individualized patrimonial jurisdictions on whose vitality it draws.

Individualized patrimonial dominion became elaborated into the right to private property. Both ideas signal the individual's right to control what falls under his power, or within his private jurisdiction. What indicates the transmutation of individualized patrimonial dominion into private property is that the nature and the extent of the individual's dominion/property become dependent on his action. Thus it is not inheritance, or the grant by an overlord of a benefice, which establishes property right. Even if an individual originally acquired his property by grant or inheritance, it is what he does with it and whether he converts it to use that counts. This construction of private property right is very clear in Locke's account. He (1965, 328–329, par. 27) makes the exercise of the individual's capacity to labor the basis of his acquisition of private property:

> Though the Earth, and all the inferior Creatures be common to all Men, yet every Man has a Property in his own Person. This no Body has any Right to but himself. The Labor of his Body, and the Work of his Hands…are properly his.

> Whatsoever then he removes out of the State that Nature hath Provided, and left it in, he hath mixed his Labor with, and joyned to it something that is his own, and thereby makes it his Property.

Moreover, Locke (1965, 342, par. 46) makes the extent of a property title dependent on the individual's effective use of his Property:

> Now of those good things which Nature hath provided in common, every one had a Right...to as much as he could use, and had a property in all that he could affect with his Labor: all that his Industry could extend to...was his...it was a foolish thing, as well as dishonest, to hoard up more than he could make use of. If he gave away a part of any body else, so that it perished not uselessly in his Possession, these he also made use of...the exceeding of the bounds of his just Property not Lying in the largeness of his Possession, but the perishing of any thing uselessly in it.

What was at first a highly restrictive limit on the extent of property right became relaxed, Locke argues (1965, 343–344, par's. 47–51), once money was introduced. This permitted investment and accumulation in an imperishable means of exchange, thus converting private property into a means of capital accumulation: "And as different degrees of Industry were apt to give Men possessions in different Proportions, so this Invention of Money gave them the opportunity to continue to enlarge them" (Locke 1965, 343, par. 48).

The individual's private property includes his jurisdiction over his household and family. Under the conditions of pre-industrial household economy, individual private property owners owned the fruits not only of their own labor but of the labor of those others who belonged to their household. These included the individual's wife, his children, and his household servants. Thus Locke (1965, 366, par. 86) speaks of "a Master of a Family with all those subordinate Relations of Wife, Children, Servants and Slaves united under the Domestick Rule of a Family." Domestic government in this sense indicates how private property represents the individualization of patrimonial dominion. It indicates also an entirely different principle of government from that involved in the democratic, political government of individuals.

It is important to appreciate that the conversion of patrimonial dominion into private property right destroyed the communal bonds which had tied the lord to those falling under his jurisdiction. Wives, children, and servants were now at serious risk of being treated as objects subject to the individual's freedom of action. This confusion of communities of persons with private property has proved to be a deep embarrassment for the natural right tradition.

The conception of individualized action in terms of private right created serious difficulty for bringing all the private property owners under the one legitimate government. On the face of it, it would appear that private dominion must exclude subjection to the jurisdiction of any other person or persons, and thus make government of private propertied individuals impossible. Both Locke and Rousseau reason that such is the case unless political government can be set up so as to represent all these individuals' wills and, in this sense, to assert a public rather than a private jurisdiction over them. Rousseau's (1968, 12) statement of the issue cannot be bettered:

> 'The problem is to find a form of association which will defend and protect with the whole common force the person and goods of each associate, and in which each, while uniting himself with all, may still obey himself alone, and remain as free as before.' This is the fundamental problem of which the social contract provides the solution.

The social contract achieves this miracle by subjecting each free agent not to the private jurisdiction of another, but to a public authority. A public authority is one which binds all by the rule of law, and administers the law impartially, while law itself represents the will of the majority within the legislature, and legislators are the elected representatives of individual actors. Locke's (1965, pp. 366–367, par. 87) statement on this is eloquent:

> Man being born...with a Title to perfect Freedom, and an uncontrolled enjoyment of all the Rights and Privileges of the Law of Nature, equally with any other Man...hath by Nature a Power, not only to preserve his Property, that is his Life, Liberty and Estate, against the Injuries and Attempts of other Men; but to judge of and punish the breaches of that Law in others, as he is persuaded the offence deserves, over with Death itself....But because no Political Society can be, nor subsist without having in itself the Power to preserve the Property, and in order thereunto punish the offenses of all those of that Society; there, and there only is Political Society, where every one of the Members hath quitted this natural power, resigned it up into the hands of the Community in all cases that excluded him not from appealing for protection to the Law established by it. And thus all private judgement of every particular Member being excluded, the Community comes to be Umpire, by settled standing Rules, indifferent, and the same to all Parties; and by Men having Authority from the Community, for the execution of those Rules, decides all the differences that may happen between any Members of that Society, concerning any matter of right; and punishes those Offences, which any member hath committed against the Society, with such Penalties as the Law has established.

Locke concludes this passage by declaring: "Those who are united into one Body, and have a common established Law and Judicature to appeal to, with

Authority to decide Controversies between them and punish offenders, are in Civil Society one with another."

This public authority is legitimate only if it has an enabling relation to private right, that is, if it provides security of property right for all individual actors who belong to the political society. Strictly speaking, the public authority cannot be a collective agent because the only real ("natural") actors are individuals. Accordingly, from natural right theory there can be very little elaboration of how a political community might be self-determining in any substantive sense. Certainly, in a world containing other political societies, a political society becomes a private property owner but this is at the not inconsiderable cost of rendering all who belong to the political society components of the national property and thereby cancelling their private right.

An important feature of the public authority relates to this last point, to which Weber (1970, 78) refers when he defines the modern state as a "human community that (successfully) claims the monopoly of the legitimate use of physical force within a given territory." In order to have a public authority which can police and secure private dominion, individuals, as Locke (1965, 368, par. 89) puts it, have to "quit everyone his Executive Power of the Law of Nature and resign it to the publick." Arguably, this significantly diminishes private right, even if it is required in order to effectively safeguard private right. Not only does this surrender of a right to use physical force (except in self-defense) qualify private right by subjecting individuals to the military force of the public authority; it also qualifies their domestic power. Unlike the *patria potestas* of ancient Rome, once individuals quit their executive power of the law of nature and resign it to the public authority they cannot exercise power of life and death over those who fall within their private, domestic jurisdictions (Locke 1965, 366, par. 86). Here the subjection of natural right to the public authority begins to establish the grounds for a genuinely universal respect for the integrity of all individual persons.

In concluding this section it will be useful to summarize the main features of natural right and, in so doing, to bring out more clearly the structure of this conception:

1 The individual becomes free to act and his own agent only as he is freed from the jurisdiction of another's will.

2 Those placed under the domestic government of a private property owner/householder—women, children, servants—cannot be regarded as individuals in their own right, even when the former have surrendered their natural executive power to the public authority.

3 However, if wives or servants leave the householder's jurisdic-

tion (see Locke's attribution of freedom of contract to them, 1965, 364, par. 82, and 365, par.s 85–86), prior to their coming under another's jurisdiction, they qualify in principle for assumption of the status of individual.

4 This is certainly true of children (sons) when they attain adulthood, and become their own householders.

5 Private right and public authority exclude each other, even though the medium through which the legitimacy of the public authority is established is the private consent of individuals.

6 Thus, extensions of the public authority's sphere of action must be viewed as likely to impede or to interfere with natural (i.e., private) right.

7 The public authority is not the same as a self-determining political community; there is no basis in the tradition of natural right for conceiving a collective freedom of action.

8 The public authority becomes an actor strictly speaking only vis-à-vis other nationally based governments, where each stands to the others as private property owners.

9 Social relations between individual actors tend to be expressed in terms of contractual exchange, because this permits trading of private property on an equal basis and so conserves the extent of each's private property.

10 It is very difficult to establish stable communities of interdependent actors on the basis of private right alone.[3]

11 Stable interdependencies are possible when social relations come under an individual's private (domestic and propertied) jurisdiction, but this entails the individual's mastery of those who fall within his jurisdiction and hence both denial of their natural equality and instrumentalization of them on behalf of the individual's private right.

12 The extent of an individual's freedom (or "power" as Hobbes calls it) is measured by the extent of his effective jurisdiction, i.e., by the amount of things he owns and number of people he commands.

13 This leads individuals to compete with one another in order both to extend their respective private property and to establish the relativities by which it makes sense to compare these extents.

14 This competitive relationship to private property is expressed in capitalist self-seeking, and, as we have seen, we have all the conditions present for there to develop the capitalist relationship between those who privately command capital (the means of production) and those whose labor power the former can exploit by bringing it under their private jurisdiction (the prerogatives of private management).

This is the basic structure of the conception of action in terms of natural right. It has certain and familiar consequences. First, since exchange relations become the prototypical expression of efforts to extend individual propertied jurisdictions without invading the dominion of other individuals, the sphere of the market becomes identified as the central arena for the expression of individual freedom. It follows that a marked economism enters into the natural right construction of action. Economic activity in the form of competitive property accumulation, market-oriented exchange, and instrumental views of others in relation to private efforts of accumulation, become prototypical aspects of free activity.

In contrast, both the state and family life have a very ambiguous standing with regard to individual freedom. This is obvious in the case of the state, for the state *qua* public authority is placed in an *interventionist* relationship to individual freedom if it does much more than umpire the competition between self-seeking individuals and thereby secure their respective natural rights. A "minimal" state as Nozick calls it (see Hoffe, 1983, 180–185) is legitimate. An interventionist state is not. Moreover, since the political community of action takes the form of a public authority (state) which empirically both transcends and is antecedent to private, natural right, it is impossible within this framework to establish the reciprocity of individual and collective levels of self-determining agency. As much as the state's legitimacy with regard to the sphere of individual action must be always problematic, the very requirement that the state transcend private interest conduces to it becoming a legal-bureaucratic machine which tends to preempt action on all levels.

The family has an ambiguous status with regard to individual freedom principally because of the embarrassment it represents in relating free men to "dependent" individuals, namely to persons who cannot express their potential agentic capacities because they are placed under the jurisdiction of the former. This dependent and subordinate status cannot be justified by the fundamental premise of natural right theories, the natural equality of all, and for explanation of it recourse must be had to reasons which fall outside the theory's framework. The exception is the case of children. The very nature of agentic freedom requires the individual to learn how to express it, to learn indeed how to be an individual. Accordingly, there is within the framework of the theory grounds for legitimizing adult authority over children where the former stand to the latter as mature actors to immature actors. At the same time adult authority is legitimate only if it educates children into the requirements of mature agency and provides for the developmental stages through which maturation of agentic capacity occurs (see Locke 1965, pp. 345–361; and for an excellent elaboration of this conception of legitimate parental authority see Blustein, 1982).

When women and servants/employees come into view as persons who fall under private jurisdictional management, there is nothing in natural right theories which can justify their subordination to private propertied individuals. Clearly, God has made some stronger and more competitive than others (Locke 1965, 346, par. 54, and 364, par. 82), but such natural inequalities are not meant to provide a basis for some coming under the jurisdiction of others.[4] Hence it is considerably easier to celebrate the freedom of action *qua* natural right if the real status of women and servants/employees can be glossed over by attributing to all adults the freedom in principle to become private property owners and their "own man." This freedom is spurious because both domestic and productive dependencies require private propertied individuals to depend on others, but since this dependence undermines their freedom *qua* natural right, it has to take the form of their bringing these others under their private dominion (Yeatman, 1984).

Within the discourse of natural right, then, a family refers to the small society of dependents falling under the patrimonial jurisdiction of an individual householder. Moreover, when the household and workplace became separated in the course of capitalist economic rationalization and industrialization, the patrimonial culture of domestic government enters into the culture of management of private economic firms.

Set against the conception of the family as a unit of domestic (private) government is another conception of the family as the sphere of education of immature actors. This identification of the family with the education of children leads in entirely different directions from the first conception of the family, and it becomes a positive basis on which the social functions of the family, state, and economy can be distinguished. The role of the public authority becomes not only to uphold the family as the unit of private government, but to support the family's educative role. This leads the state to provide a number of services to support this role, and to complement it with the provision of rationalized (and, hence, professionalized) modes of education.

Once the state enters the picture by regulating, supporting and complementing privately based parental modes of education of children, there is considerable potential for its role to clash with private right. Moreover, by elaborating what children must learn in order to become mature agents, and by providing a range of different services in support of this learning and the bodily health and vigor of children, the state's activities imply that the conditions of agentic right depend much more on a shared culture oriented to self-determining agency and, thus, on some kind of agentic community than natural right theories can acknowledge. Note also that precisely because private property and its extent depend on the *action* of individuals, there is a premium placed on the necessity of educating *all* individuals in the requirements of action: otherwise natural potential may be unreasonably fettered and restricted by uneven and unjustifiable distributions of access to education. This premium comes to place on the state considerable responsibility in ensuring equality of opportunity in access to education and to all other conditions of action.

Beyond Natural Right: The Division of Labor in Society

As a complex, industrialized society developed, the household and economic production became differentiated. Since productive units became relatively large-scale and increasingly complex organizations, they were obviously trans-household in character. In this context it became very much more problematic to view the master-servant relation as a model for the management-labor relation. To be sure, private ownership of firms seemed to warrant bringing firms and those who worked for them within the private jurisdictional control of the property owners concerned, but it was difficult to conceive this control in terms of an individualized patrimonial dominion. This was especially so when ownership itself became shared and thereby assumed a collective character. Finally, as aspects of the management of firms became professionalized, it was increasingly difficult to reconcile the culture of professional authority with that of patrimonial authority.

For theorists like Emile Durkheim (1964) it was perfectly clear that modern industrial and occupational/professional life could not be understood or framed in terms of natural right theory. The theory cannot grasp the inherently collective features of modern industrial and professional life. For Durkheim this collective character is most evident in the complex web of interdependencies between both distinct, specialized branches of the division of labor in society, and within any particular profession or industry. No one private jurisdiction can cover and thus control the increasing scale of the social division of labor. Accordingly, the appropriate institutional expression of the modern division of labor is the corporate or professional group. Professional groups link up all those belonging to a particular industry or profession, and represent the corporate interest of that industry or profession within a national legislative assembly. It is clear that this corporative type of democratic socialism is treating the institution of private property as essentially anachronistic.[5]

For Durkheim, as for more recent advocates of industrial democracy, it makes no sense to subject the professional or occupational agency of individuals to private patrimonial control. The vigor and dynamics, and indeed for Durkheim, the morality, of the division of labor in society depend on each individual being free to act in occupational or professional terms. This statement (Durkheim, 1965, 131) is typical of his reasoning:

> ...on the one hand, each one depends as much more strictly on society as labor is more divided; and, on the other, the activity of each is as much more personal as it is specialized. Doubtless, as circumscribed as it is, it is never completely original. Even in the exercise of our occupation, we conform to usages, to practices which are common to our whole professional brotherhood. But, even in this instance, the yoke that we submit to is much less heavy than when society completely controls us, and it leaves much more place open for the free play of our initiative. Hence, then, the individuality of all grows at the same time as that of its parts. Society becomes more capable of collective movement, at the same time that each of its elements has more freedom of movement.

Here it is clear that Durkheim intuits the reciprocal relation between the self-determination of a political community of action and the self-determination of individual actors who belong within this community.

There are, however, serious problems with this corporative theory of action. Before we turn to them it is important to emphasize that Durkheim's status as a theorist of the division of labor in society may be taken as representative of how most theorists in the last half of the nineteenth century, including Marx, conceived the nature of social action. The sphere of social action concerns the sphere of interdependencies which a complex, technically advanced division of labor in society involves. For both Marx and Durkheim the truth of modern productive-creative agency lies more in these interdependencies than it does in the private ownership of productive firms and market capacities.

For them, as for others influenced by the classical political economists, civil society is this sphere of social action structured by the interdependencies of a complex division of labor. Significantly, civil society thereby loses the political connotation it had enjoyed when Locke and Rousseau made "civil society" synonymous with what Locke called "political society" (for extended discussion and critique of this shift in the meaning of civil society, see Wolin, 1961).

This construction of civil society radically simplifies the terrain of action. Since the family is no longer a site for professional or productive activity, it tends to drop out of the picture and to become taken for granted as operating normally in its reproductive functions. Moreover, since the totality of specialized productive and occupational activity comprises a self-sufficient system of interdependencies, the regulative role of the state can easily appear as a residual with regard to the social division of labor and the system of activity it connotes.

This construction of the sphere of action maintains the economistic bias of the earlier one. It is true that, with "the division of labor in society," we have departed from the classical natural right territory, but have we moved away altogether? When individual action becomes identified with occupational or professional action, there is no reason why individuals should be collectively rather than privately oriented to the interdependencies in which they are involved. Within this sphere of action it makes as much sense for individuals to be oriented to their private and competitive advantage as it does for them to be oriented to patterns of cooperation and shared advantage. What balance they strike between the two, and whether they instrumentalize their knowledge of these patterns of cooperation on behalf of their private advantage, is up to them.

Even if theorists of the division of labor in society argue—as do Marx and Durkheim—that the potential for the self-determination of the society which comprises a productive/occupational system cannot be realized until the culture of possessive individualism (Macpherson, 1962) is replaced by a social orientation which is expressed in the conscious planning and direction of this system, there is nothing in their conception of the nature of action which can provide anchorage for this idea. Indeed it is questionable whether the division of labor in society can support a political community at all. The scope of the former becomes global, inter- and transnational. It elides all boundaries which historically provide the bases for political communities (Walzer, 1983, 31–64). The division of labor may become the basis of a "social system," but a social system is not the same thing as a "political community." A social system is ruled by the interdependence of functions and by the instrumentally rational culture of orientation of actors to these functions. It is not meaningful to attribute the project of self-determination to a social system, as it is with regard to a political community. The political community, however, must be a definitely bounded community of citizens (for further discussion of this point, see Chapter Five). As Walzer (1983, 63) argues:

> The theory of distributive justice begins...with an account of membership rights. It must vindicate at one and the same time the (limited) right of closure, without which there could be no communities at all, and the political inclusiveness of the existing communities. For it is only as members somewhere that men and women can hope to share in all the other goods—security, wealth, honor, office, and power—that communal life makes possible.

With "the division of labor in society," it is true to say that we have gone beyond the classical and patrimonial theory of natural right. In a sense the substitute turns out to be a purer form of natural right. Occupational or professional action, and civil society, as the sphere of action, come to center stage stripped of all patrimonial tradition and able to be oriented in terms of a pure instrumental rationality. Natural right comes to be reinterpreted as functional right.

Functional right can support equal opportunity and a meritocracy, but it is very limited with regard to developing a self-determining political community of citizens. Functional right marginalizes all nonproductive action: it thereby marginalizes the spheres of action and citizenship which the state and family life respectively denote, as it marginalizes all who cannot count as productive. These are not actors (individuals) in terms of "the division of labor in society."[6]

Beyond Natural Right: Social Citizenship and the Welfare State

The differentiation of the household and economic production involves also the differentiation of the household and the structures of government. Households can no longer be regarded as "little commonwealths" where much of the business of government is delegated to domestic governors under whose jurisdiction most members of the society fall. This delegation is supplemented by local units of government which link households together: the parish and the parish church. The differentiation of the household from both economic activity and the business of government provides the basis for it to become identified increasingly with the inner world of family life. The household is redefined in terms of the value of domesticity, and it becomes a "home."

The structures of government, on the other hand, increasingly become identified with national co-ordination of monitoring of population movements, and national regulation of goods and services. Government, in short, takes on the features of the trans-household and trans-locality administration of what has now become a complex web of relationships and ties on a vastly increased scale. The tasks of government in this context force it to assume the characteristics of the modern state and of the complex administrative apparatus involved in the tasks of the modern state. Not least of these tasks is its provision of structures of legal and administrative regulation and of various services which underpin the national economy, on the one hand, and the family life of its citizens, on the other.

Families, in this context, come to be viewed as units of consumption. Insofar as the health and well-being of adults and children depend on families functioning as effective units of consumption, the state provides regulation and services which support family functioning in this respect. Family-based parenting tends to be viewed in terms of women's effective nurturance and nourishment of children so that they become healthy and mentally alert adults. The state develops services which help mothers become better informed as to their children's needs for nourishment and, in the case of poorer families, the state provides supplements to family means of consumption. Moreover the state develops use of a national school system as an instrument of quality control with regard to the care and education of children. Once the state proceeds to develop a universal social security system for all who fall under its jurisdiction, the structures of the welfare state are effectively complete.

Against this backdrop, natural right theory appears as irrelevant and anachronistic. It is clear that in an empirical sense the state has become much more than the minimal state of natural right theory. As Hoffe (1983,185) puts it:

> The modern state has assumed responsibility for the basic framework of society in which its citizens live. It determines working conditions and provides for old age, sickness and accidents; it tries to curb unemployment and inflation and to encourage economic growth; it implements cultural, educational and scientific policy, energy and transport policy and lays down directives for the protection of the environment and town and country planning.

> This development, whereby the state has taken on an increased number of duties, has occurred over the past hundred years; most of the time it has happened naturally and, so it would seem, for good reasons. The development of the modern social welfare state, with its vast network of services and obligations, is an answer to experiences of oppression in recent history, resulting from a world changed by capitalism, technology and industrialization.

The argument is not simply that, empirically speaking, the complexity and all-pervasive reach of the modern state is left unaccounted for by theories based in the idea of natural right. After all, such theories could be used to make this development of the state into an interventionist one appear illegitimate, and without any normative authority with regard to the bases of right. Use of natural right theories in this way informs the contemporary politics of neoconservatism and the new right. When it can be shown that the interventionist state has not only fostered but instituted the rights of individuals, and that real as opposed to ideal rights depend on such positive state intervention, natural right theories and the politics they help to inspire are rendered powerless to account for these things. If it turns out that a conception of state-institutionalized rights allow more persons to be included in the culture of rights, as right-bearing individuals, than natural-rights theories do, then the latter appear a less universalistic theory of right than do the former. Let us look at this more closely.

T. H. Marshall (1977, 78–79), one of the great theoretical exponents of the welfare state, distinguishes three components of rights: civil, political, and social. He (1977, 78) defines the civil component as "composed of the rights necessary for individual freedom—liberty of the person, freedom of speech, thought and faith, the right to own property and to conclude valid contracts, and the right to justice." The political component involves "the right to participate in the exercise of political power, as a member of a body invested with political authority or as an elector of the members of such a body." Together these civil and political rights constitute the familiar terrain of natural right. Marshall (1977, 78–79) defines "the social element" as "the whole range from the right to a modicum of economic welfare and security to the right to share to the full in the social heritage and to live the life of a civilized being according to the standards prevailing in the community." He adds: "The institutions most closely connected with it are the educational system and the social services."

Social rights transcend the framework of natural right, and cannot be accommodated by this framework. Social rights involve the provision of a basic level of material support and education for individuals so that they can act, and conceive themselves as self-determining. Education is particularly crucial because without being trained in the skills and knowledge necessary for reflexive participation in social life and for a critical relationship to authority, an individual cannot be an effectively self-determining agent. As Marshall (1977, 889) argues:

> The right to education is a genuine social right of citizenship, because the aim of education during childhood is to shape the future adult. Fundamentally it should be regarded, not as the right of the child to go to school, but as the right of the adult to have been educated.

Social rights are a prerequisite if civil and political rights are to be real and effective. If social rights require the positive intervention of the state, civil and political rights are now anchored in a quite different framework from that of natural right.

This new framework is identified with the core value of *citizenship*. The discourse of citizenship is universal: it extends the status of "individual" to all who fall under the state's jurisdiction and all become counted as members of the state as a self-determining political community. Within the framework of citizenship we are invited to consider and debate the conditions on which all persons can be admitted to the status of individual citizens, who enjoy real and effective capacity to participate in all aspects of the society and polity to which they belong. Moreover, the framework of citizenship shifts us beyond a "Political Society"/minimal state which is perched, as legislator and magistrate, above the real stuff of living and relationships. Citizenship requires the state to become anchored in the real space and time co-ordinates of the everyday life of its members. In effect, citizenship makes the state the practical embodiment of the collective policy responses required by a Maslovian hierarchy of needs where the goal is to make it possible for all to be oriented as self-actualizing individuals.

This not only sends the state into the corners of hitherto private household jurisdictions but brings out onto the table for policy consideration a much more thorough map of the requirements of social life. This is a social map which transcends the market-oriented mediations of the division of labor in society, which is limited to the occupational division of labor and the division of labor between the propertied and propertyless. On the social map of citizenship, activities such as "caring" for the elderly and the disabled (Finch and Groves, 1983), and the domestic maintenance of children and adults at home, become salient for the state.

Social rights, accordingly, bring within the ambit of citizenship those whom natural right had left subject to private patriarchal dominion: women, children, and household servants. Social rights not only focus attention on the preconditions for full employment of political and civil rights; they provide also a framework within which it is quite clear that the state constitutes all rights: political, civil, social.

Durkheim's argument in *Professional Ethics and Civic Morals* (1957) is important here. Durkheim proposes that the individuality which rights enable is a "moral" individuality made possible only by the individual person's maturation within the moral community of any one particular society. The cognitive, moral, and affective components of individuality all must develop so as to constitute an autonomous individual agent capable of bearing rights. These components derive not from a natural individuality but from one whose internal life has been developed and enriched by the internalization of a cognitive, moral, and affective education provided by other agents with whom the individual has interacted.[7] That this education develops an autonomous individual, who seeks to be a self-determining agent in relation to a community of self-determining agents, depends on a shared culture which is oriented to core values such as individual rights, to democratic participation, and to the institutions required to uphold them. Development of moral individuality depends, then, both on a shared democratic culture and on the positive institutionalization of this culture.

Durkheim is quite clear that if rights are not positively instituted they do not exist. He is equally clear that the state is the vehicle of the institutionalization of rights. Thus Durkheim (1957, 64) argues: "It is only through the State that individualism is possible, although it cannot be the means of making it a reality, except in certain precise conditions." In a further passage (1957, 65) he explains:

> If indeed we work on the premise that the rights of the individual are not *ipso facto* his at birth; that they are not inscribed in the nature of things with such certainty as warrants the State in endorsing them and promulgating them; that, on the contrary, the rights have to be won from the opposing forces that deny them; that the State alone is qualified to play this part—then it cannot keep to the functions of supreme arbiter and of administrator of an entirely prohibitive justice, as the utilitarian or Kantian individualism would have it. No, the State must deploy energies equal to those for which it has to provide a counterbalance. It must ever permeate all those secondary groups of family, trade and professional association, Church, regional areas and so on...which tend...to absorb the personality of their members.

If individual rights require the state's supervision of all secondary groups so as to ensure they do not violate the rights of the individual, secondary groups themselves must be free to question the state's activities, to debate state policies, and to present their views to state policy-makers. Otherwise, there is no force sufficient to check the state's potential for absorbing the personalities of its members. Durkheim identifies (1957, 69) the mission of the modern state with its "tendency...to ensure the most complete individuation that the state of society will allow of." This is a radical dismissal of natural right theories:

> What lies at the base of individual right is not the notion of the individual as he is, but the way in which society puts the right into practice, looks upon it and appraises it. What matters is not what the individual is, but how much he counts and on the other hand, what he ought to be. The reason why he has more or fewer, certain rights and not others, is not that he is consulted in a particular way; it is because society attributes this or that importance to him and attaches a higher or a lower value to what concerns him....Those who believe in that theory of natural right think they can make a final distinction between what is and what is not a right. However, a closer study will show that in reality the dividing line they think they can draw is certainly not definite and depends entirely on the state of public opinion (Durkheim, 1957, 67).

It is important to underline the radical and critical force of this last claim, especially as it will seem to the proponents of natural right to represent a dangerous relativizing of the basis of right. Durkheim's claim makes all of us as a self-determining political community responsible for what rights are, for who has them, and in respect of which arenas of social action. This is a democratic perspective which enables us to be open to criticism that "our" rights are so constructed as to minimize or to exclude those of others. This is not so with natural right theories. The very absolutism of the basis of right in these theories precludes dialogue and debate with regard to the interactional features of rights.

This statist and sociological theory of right permits Durkheim (1957, 64) to see the state as the liberator of women and children: "It is the state that has rescued the child from patriarchal domination and from family tyranny; it is the state that has freed the citizen from feudal groups and later from communal groups; it is the state that has liberated the craftsman and his master from guild tyranny." The empirical basis for this proposition is incontestable. The interventionist welfare state has been a positive and empowering influence for women and children as self-determining agents. Indeed, since the tradition of natural right has never embraced the rights of women and children, it is very much easier in their case than in the case of men to see that the state constitutes their political, civil, and social rights.

The welfare state, then, seems to secure universal citizenship for all. It has to examine, even if it cannot resolve, the fundamental contradiction inherent in its makeup between a universal citizenship based in social rights, on the one hand, and the social inequalities which are caused by privately oriented economic action in civil society, on the other. This contradiction is the thrust of T. H. Marshall's (1977) lectures on "Citizenship and Social Class."[8] The bringing into light of this contradiction is a major step forward.

Finally, the culture of citizenship of the welfare state begins to explore issues of diversity and difference with regard to what citizenship means and how it is to be expressed. If women and children, as well as male householders, are to have rights, rights and citizen participation must be conceived in differentiated ways so as to permit them to be exercised across political, economic, familial, and other arenas, and to be exercised by immature as well as mature individual actors.

The interventionist welfare state represents the development of a universal culture of citizenship, but there is a major flaw in the way that this culture is institutionalized in the welfare state. This weakness is indicated in the very language of making "the state" stand in for the political community. It is not clear these are the same thing; neoconservatives have exploited this weakness by arguing that the state has become captive to special interest groups and to the "class" interest of its bureaucratic functionaries. Here Hoffe's comment (1983, 186) is insightful:

> The minimal-state concept is attractive in that it protects individuals and groups from the Moloch state. But we should not overlook the major problems of modern industrial society, starting with social issues. The social state came into being in order to ensure that freedom is truly guaranteed to everyone and is not just an empty word to many, especially those who possess nothing. We can only dispense with the social state if we are prepared to give up taking the concept of true freedom seriously. We must not forget...that the social state is an 'operational' state, requiring increased state intervention, through which it interferes directly or indirectly with the freedom of individuals. The modern state is therefore in a dilemma: the more it advances towards the social realization of freedom, the more is the use of this same freedom controlled by the state.

Neoconservatives would have us revert to the natural right tradition and the minimal state concept. This would be a retrogressive move from the point of view of developing universal structures of citizenship. If we are to move forward, however, we must treat the *étatisme* of the welfare state critically and reflectively.

This leads us to a deeper understanding of the nature and limits of the welfare state. Marshall's discernment of the contradiction between social rights and social class glosses over how this contradiction has become embodied in the very culture and institutions of the welfare state itself. Donzelot's (1979) analysis is more instructive here. From the outset, Donzelot argues, there was built into the welfare state a basic distinction of status: *contract* as distinct from *tutelage*.

What this means is that if you can make it in market terms—gain access to labor or capital markets in such a fashion as to become an economically independent individual—you are classified as "middle class," and are able to "contract into" any of the services you want and are able to buy. If, on the other hand, you are not able to establish a market-based independence, you can get access to subsidized or public housing, various forms of income support, public health and other services, but not on conditions of your choosing. Instead you are placed under the tutelage of state officials and state-sponsored professional service deliverers, who determine whether you fit the criteria of eligibility for state support, what your real needs are, and how and whether they are to be fulfilled. Services which by their nature—for instance, the psychoanalytically oriented therapies—depend on contractual choice are denied to the clients of welfare state tutelage.

Moreover, as feminist analyses (Pateman, 1989) have shown, this distinction between contract and tutelage inevitably takes a patriarchalist form. By historical position and social advantage, those most fitted for "contract" are adult men, while the dependence on patriarchal domestic government of women and children makes them obvious candidates for welfare state "tutelage." This is also true of ethnic or racial groups who have been identified historically with domestic or household service: Blacks in the United States and Aboriginals in Australia, for example.

The distinction between contract and tutelage ensures that social rights cannot be instituted in a genuinely universal way. Even when, formally speaking, social rights and the services they inform are instituted universally—as in, for example, a public school system—there must be room left for contract and room thus also for a privately sponsored school system. This ensures that the public service takes on tutelage connotations as distinct from the private service which is associated with freedom of contract. The privately sponsored service can end up with heavy state subsidies—as with the Australian school system—while at the same time the public service is allowed to run down, ensuring its identification with disadvantaged groups.

The welfare state has been structured so as to accommodate the prior culture and institution of natural right. The consequence is to force the welfare state to appear as a morally less advanced principle (tutelage) in relation to contractually expressed freedom. This has the additional consequence of requiring the state to assume features which bring it closer to the culture of authority which characterizes patrimonial dominion than to the democratic culture of a political community. In short, the *étatisme* of the welfare state is required by its accommodation to the institutions of natural right.

Beyond Natural Right: The Conditions for Universal Citizenship

If we are to advance we must move beyond natural right. We can neither adapt nor modify this idea so as to permit a genuinely universal citizenship. Natural right entails a primitive conception of individuality, which brings with it an unresolvable tension between public and private claims, between the values of individuality and sociality. Moreover this "natural" individuality cannot be universalized so as to include all. Some are more "individual" than others, and the vast majority falls under the private control of those who are more effectively individual than most.

We cannot move beyond natural right unless we can develop a genuinely alternative conception of what it means to be an individual, which permits all to be equally individual. We have the means to do this. Both recent feminist and object relations theorizing—sometimes conjoined as in Chodorow (1985)—permit us to understand the interactional basis and dynamics of individuality. The self is a relational self: a self capable of autonomy has an autonomous self-concept, and this self-concept can come into being only as it has been fostered and encouraged by the object relations in which the self has been engaged (Miller, 1981, 1983, 1984).

The idea of autonomy in object relations theory is a radical idea in the context both of natural right and welfare state traditions. An autonomous self is not one who masters and disciplines his "impulses" and feelings so as to instrumentalize himself on behalf of an effective course of self-seeking in the marketplace. As Levine (1985) argues, this form of self-seeking actually denies, or as Freud puts it, represses the self. Capitalist self-seeking depends, in this sense, on violations to the self as well as on the exploitation and instrumentalization of the selves of others. Instead, an autonomous self is one who experiences himself or herself as an integral, feeling and sentient self, the authenticity and thus autonomy of whose expressions require authorization by this integral self. Miller's (1981, 33) concept of a "healthy self-feeling" is appropriate here:

> I understand a healthy self-feeling to mean the unquestioned certainty that the feelings and wishes one experiences are a part of one's self. This certainty is not something one can gain upon reflection; it is there like one's own pulse, which one does not notice as long as it functions normally.

An autonomous self can come into being only if, from birth, he or she is permitted to experience his or her feelings and sentience within the safe presence of mature persons who fully accept this emergent self (Winnicott, 1965). A person can actualize his or her true self only if permitted and encouraged to do so by respect and love for this self by others (Miller, 1981, 32–34, on the conditions for a "healthy narcissism"). This means that the individual (as a child and thereafter) is not instrumentalized on behalf of the needs of others, and, specifically, that those who parent a child do not instrumentalize him or her to meet their needs.

Throughout her work, Miller makes the point that if, from infancy, one has been respected as a separate self, one will have no difficulty respecting the integrity of other selves. In particular, precisely because one has not developed a "false" self in adaptation to the wishes of one's parents, one can experience oneself as a separate person and see others as separate persons. This permits a genuine recognition of the existence of oneself within a society of selves, and permits also acceptance of the diversity of views and perceptions which all those individuals have to offer. The culture of citizenship which autonomous selves can develop is one which embodies this respect for the separateness, integrity, and diversity of selves. This culture cannot assume authoritarian features, for, clearly, autonomous selves are refractory characters. They experience a positive relationship between their own individuality and that of others. Since they understand that their own sense of self depends on ongoing positive encouragement and affirmation from others, autonomous selves are generous and community-oriented in their relationship to the shared conditions of their existence. However, they reject all forms of tutelage (and thus the old paternalism of welfare state "compassion"), for contract is a crucial mediation of social relations for autonomous selves. They need to choose all that they do. Again, this is a choice quite different from the privately oriented choices of natural right-oriented individuals. The autonomous self chooses in ways that involve his or her understanding of his or her social connectedness and of how the capacity to choose is enhanced by the wealth (the social capital) which he or she shares with the political community of selves to which he or she belongs.

To elaborate this alternative conception we would need to see how it recasts the family, the state, and civil society. This must be left for another occasion. In closing, I wish to emphasize that we do not have an alternative to natural right theory, and that it is urgent that we begin to work on it. This will involve us in conserving the positive features of the individualism which natural right denotes, and resituating them within a self-determining political community of self-determining individuals.

5

Minorities and the Politics of Difference

I

Traditions of modern citizenship are tied to the notion that, for citizenship to be possible, there must be an independent, self-determining community of citizens. At first sight, there appears to be an inevitable and logical linkage between claims for self-determination at the level of the individual citizen and those for self-determination at the level of the political community to which he or she belongs. However, the way that this community understands itself, constructs its integrity, and proceeds to institutionalize itself cannot be left unquestioned. As political theorists begin to discern (e.g. Hindess, 1992), this is a community which understands its integrity and viability to be dependent on clear-cut boundaries delineating who belongs and who does not. It is a community which requires an identity of being from those who belong, and, at the same time, a non-identity of being in respect of those who do not belong.

Community and difference are mutually exclusive terms in this conception of a citizenship community (see also Yuval-Davis, 1991). As we shall see, this requires not simply the exclusion of "outsiders," but the systemic exclusion of many who are situated within the social relations of the citizenship community. We are at an historical juncture, one at which this issue of exclusion has become pressing. Those who are excluded from within are developing a politics of voice and representation which makes visible these internal exclusions and their systemic character. Those who are excluded from without represent claims on global redistribution of citizen status most often through claims on migration to the affluent citizenship communities of the "First World." A related phenomenon: globalized patterns of movement which follow on, for example, the development of integrated, free-trade blocs (e.g. Europe, the United States with Canada and Mexico, Australia and New Zealand) lead to the presence in one citizen community of many more or less legal residents with important affiliations to another citizen community.

For the traditions of citizenship which we inherit, the quality of being a community is made to originate in a shared order of being. With modern citizenship, this shared order of being is a secular, rational concept. "The public" comes into being through reason, as that which is shared by the individuals who comprise the public. Thus the *ethnos* of this community is one which is distinguished by a specific, jurisdictional reason. It is expressed as the rational, legal order which Weber identified as the principle of legitimation of the modern state.

It is important to appreciate the insight which liberalism affords us in respect of the way that the modern citizenship community is conceived. In his *Second Treatise of Government*, John Locke accords individuals freedom to leave the particular Commonwealth into which they are born. As long as they enjoy the advantages afforded by a particular Commonwealth—e.g. access to property right—they are to submit to its conditions (*Second Treatise*, ch. 6, par. 73); however, if they are willing to forfeit these advantages, they have right of exit. Here difference and a community of governance are made mutually exclusive terms.

Kukathas (1992), in an interesting discussion of "cultural rights," brings out the logic of this classical liberal premise. He grounds cultural rights in the form of a group cultural identity, in which the identity of the group takes precedence over and subordinates that of the individual by arguing that an individual always has right of exit. The two alternatives are then: either the subordination of self to the identity and claims of the group; or, individual exit and choice, perhaps, of life in the modern city, where group cultural rights can no longer be effectively policed.

One may point out to Kukathas that this right of exit is effectively denied to the vulnerable members of cultural groups—women and children, for example—but the prior point concerns precisely their condition of vulnerability, and how it follows from the liberal construction of group identity. For the logic of Kukathas's analysis is to bring out the illiberal character of the liberal construction of the group. The liberal's methodological individualism requires him to treat the group as though it were an individual, a corporate individual in this case. Just as with the liberal's "natural" individual, the group is accorded a clearly bounded integrity and the coherence of a monorational willing agency. This is the kind of agency that requires to be expressed as singular, unambiguous, and, preferably, reasoned purpose. It does not easily accommodate ambivalences, ambiguities, contradictions, incoherencies, multiplicities of intention and purpose. It becomes clear that the liberal conception of the group requires the group to assume an authoritarian character: there has to be a headship of the group which represents its homogeneity of purpose by speaking with the one, authoritative voice. For this to occur, the politics of voice and representation latent within the heterogeneity of perspectives and interests must be suppressed. Necessarily, then, this is a construction of the group and of its authority which requires, first, a legitimation device which permits those who are accorded full status as individual members of the group to subordinate their individuality to the public authority of the group. This fiction is some version of the Social Contract. Second, this is a construction which requires of those whom these individuals master—women, children, servants—a subsumption of their individuality within that of their masters. These categories of persons have no right of exit.

The liberal alternative of individual contractual freedom and monorational, public authoritarianism mask the subsumption within the former of domestic despotism and the way that this functions to occlude the authoritarianism of the public authority. If this is the grounding of "cultural rights" it is one which has more in common with national socialism than it has with the contemporary politics of voice and representation. This politics contests precisely the unicity of the group, the coherence of the putative common culture, the very idea that the group has a bounded, coherent identity which can be expressed as the one voice. It is a politics which opens up the group itself to its internal lines of dissent and contested domination, and to its own historically specific contradictions, ambiguities, ambivalences, "forgettings" and repressions. This opening up has a parallel in how the individuals who open up this politics understand themselves: they are selves no longer required to conform to the liberal model of self. These are selves which understand their integrity to lie indeed in the historically specific dynamics of their own contradictions, incoherencies, ambivalences, repressions, and in the intersection of these with the contingencies and changes of the histories within which they find themselves situated.

The politics of voice and representation, by adopting a very different starting point from that of our modern and ancient traditions of citizenship, brings out their commonality, their subscription to some notion of *being* as the grounds of membership of a citizen community. "Being" signifies an origin or foundation from which the identity of the community as well as that of the individual derives. Such a foundationalist approach necessarily forecloses the historical pragmatics of a politics of voice and representation. Where this politics introduces the pragmatics of historically contingent negotiated settlements in relation to a polyvocal and non-consensual citizen community, the foundationalist approach implies a pre-existent totality to which the citizen community must conform. Where the former abandons the givens of originary being and works with the givens of historically contingent specificities, the latter always assumes the inevitably utopian orientation to an ideal implied in the logic of being.

Such an ontological approach to identity is one which explains how it is that such an individualistic approach to social life as liberalism is so self-denying. For a self to express itself as univocal, clear, and monorational purpose, it must submit itself to a harsh and rigorous regime of self-mastery. Not only does this regime require the self to "other" vast areas of its own internal complexity, but to "other" those subjects whose presence it requires in order to make its will socially visible. This is a self which is compelled to "forget" that it others both parts of itself and other subjects. In order to maintain the fiction of its ontological givenness as a coherent, bounded self, it must proceed to forget this forgetting (my debt to Lyotard's *Heidegger and the "jews"* will be obvious).

This double forgetting clearly authorizes a terror both over self and others. This terror haunts all ontological accounts of citizenship, both ancient and those of modern republicanism, liberalism, and communism.

A non- or perhaps, better, a post-ontological approach to citizenship is suggested in what I and others are terming a politics of difference. Here an openly contested politics of voice and representation makes it very difficult to sustain ontological orientations for it becomes very evident that any one of them is in a highly contested relation to others. More significantly, it becomes evident also that these ontological orientations are *internally* contested, and that their "being" is more a creature of contingent history than it is of some pre-historical point of origin. By bringing out the way that all constructions of homogeneous community or identity depend on systemic exclusions, on domination, these internal contestations make it all the more difficult to forget the forgetting of those who are othered by assertions of self and group identity. Moreover, the self/other dialectic surely changes when assertion of self is no longer predicated on requiring the self to be a tightly-bounded, coherent, separate self.

This is the beginnings of exploration of such an alternative account of citizenship, one that fits Iris Young's (1990b, 10) vision of "a heterogeneous public that acknowledges and affirms group differences." As will be clear, a citizenship politics has to be an identity politics, one that involves competing accounts of the grounds of identity not just of the group or collectivity concerned but of the individual self. The valorization of difference which this politics authorizes has implications for how a *res publica* is structured and distributed. For any citizenship community to be possible it must be expressed through and resourced by a *res publica*. In this case, the *res publica* must work with and resource differentiation.

II

In recent years, feminists, among others, have been placed in a difficult situation. Having developed a critique of the exclusions of women that are inherent rather than accidental features of modern discourses of citizenship, they have seemed to warrant, even to legitimize, the abandonment of these discourses, an abandonment which has been implicated in the economic-rationalist substitution of the market for the polity as a distributive mechanism. Indeed, there are those of us who think that the abandonment of the discourse of citizenship by dominant groups at this point of time is their response to the increasing effectiveness of claims on citizenship by groups historically identified as "other," or, in more contemporary parlance, as "minorities."

In ways that I shall elaborate, oppressed groups have developed a normative conception of citizenship that is able to take up and value difference. This conception is opposed to the modern liberal and republican conceptions of citizenship which are predicated on the idea of a civic community as one which is homogeneous and monocultural (monorational, if you will). In these conceptions, in order to become a citizen, individuals have to show that their social circumstance qualifies them to adopt the universal, general point of view, one which brackets out particularity, difference, and the vicissitudes of embodiment. It is not just women who are excluded from the modern civic ideal. All who have been "othered" by the assertion of a disembodied, rationalist principle of generality (whether this is that of the rational state or of market transaction) are excluded from this ideal. These others include all whose bodies require special provision—who are constituted as dis-abled in respect of the norm—and all who are regarded by their occupational placement or culture as unable to attain the impersonal, rational and disembodied practices of the modal citizen: children, older people, and racial and ethnic minorities identified with powerless, dirty and poorly paid positions in the social division of labor. This occupational placement has historical roots in the way in which modern civilization necessarily operated to divide the world into those who were the givers of civilization and those who required to be given civilization.

Before I proceed, let me exemplify the ways in which liberal, republican and welfare state discourses of modern citizenship constitute those who become the excluded others in relation to those who are constituted as citizens. Liberal discourse requires self- or privately-oriented individuals to find what it is that they have in common in order to institute a public authority which upholds this common interest as the rule of law. In order to establish their common interest they have to bracket out their private or particular interests. This brackets out all that is particular about individuals, not only their self-interested aspects, but all that is unique and personal about them, including the social relations of private households. As feminist critics in particular have remarked it is a primitive kind of individuality that is in view when it permits a conception of what individuals have in common to be a homogeneity of interest. Stated differently, the *res publica* in the liberal vision cannot assume substantive features precisely because it brackets out all that belongs to the substantive social life of individuals. Like the market, it admits only the formally commensurable features of individual lives. The liberal construction of citizenship requires an other who will bear the substantively individual aspects of individuality, an other who will stand in for personal/private life and all that belongs to it by way of passion, desire, embodiment, and commitment. Thus, as Joan Landes, Carole Pateman and others have shown, liberal discourse invents "women" as the other to whom the masculine citizens can delegate their private, personal being.

Republican discourse depends on a vision of a substantive civic community that is achieved through rational consensus. This is a participatory ideal of citizenship, where citizens are accorded responsibility for the life and health of the self-determining polity. Habermas develops the participatory democratic values of the new left, and gives new life to republican discourse, when he theorizes the conditions for communicative interaction unconstrained by domination, and thus able to assume genuinely dialogical qualities. However, as Iris Young and other feminist critics have remarked, the regulative ideal of this participatory and dialogical process is a monocultural reason. Habermas assumes that rational process will lead to rational consensus. This assumption is possible only if substantive differences are bracketed out of this dialogical process, for such differences introduce a necessarily irreducible plurality of perspectives—reasons rather than reason, to paraphrase Lyotard. As feminist critiques of Rousseau have demonstrated, the republican ideal, by requiring a reason which bracketed out the heterogeneity of social life, necessarily othered women, children and primitives to represent all that thereby became impossible to admit within this conception of reason. Women, children and primitives became identified with the irrational or non-rational, with conditions of social life that are not subject to rational control—all that became constructed as instinctual, intuitive, impulsive, or as ungoverned aspects of embodiment and mind. In particular, the othering of the primitive represents the way in which this conception of reason, monocultural as it is, separates itself from substantive cultural differences.

As to the welfare state discourse of citizenship, it generated a dualistic distinction between those who can achieve independent status as freely contracting individuals via market activity, and those who for various reasons are unable to achieve this status, and for whom, therefore, special provision must be made. In short, as feminist critiques have again shown, the welfare state discourse of citizenship was predicated on a distinction between contract and tutelage. Inevitably, this meant that "citizens" who received their social entitlements by way of public income support, public housing, etc., found themselves in a compromised relationship to the administration of these services. This administration was and is designed so as to impress on them their client status, their lack of contractual freedom, of choice. The welfare state discourse of citizenship was (and is) predicated on a dualism of independence and dependency (see also Smith, 1989–1990). This discourse comes out of the same complex of values as the modern republican and liberal discourses of citizenship. They all identify the model citizen with the formal individuality of a rationally-oriented, freely contracting subject. For such an identification to work, all that is substantively needy about our lives, which makes us interdependent with each other, has to be bracketed out. Again, welfare state discourse invents an other on whom this interdependency, conceptualized as dependency, is projected: women, who thereby become associated with all who are substantively needy (husbands, children, elderly parents, disabled relatives, etc.).

There is a republican dimension of welfare state discourse, recently discussed by Hindess (1992), and clearly expressed in the progressivist ideas of the 1920's. Progressivism, like T.H. Marshall's conception of social citizenship, assumed that citizens require a collective structure of consumption to uphold their capacity to participate in the common culture or civilization of their society. It is this participation that makes the society self-determining. Hence, public libraries and other cultural institutions enter what is conceived as the *res publica* in order to resource and develop this active citizenry. Lyndon Johnson's "Great Society" was perhaps one of the last echoes of this kind of conception of the welfare state—this was the period when "Head Start" informed the development of "Sesame Street" as an educational program which was oriented inclusively to, especially, socially disadvantaged children.

Again it becomes clear that social citizenship invents its other as those who are constituted as "special" because disadvantaged, deviant in relation to a norm. Social citizenship is predicated on an assimilationist ideal, where the goal is to normalize those who have marginal relationships to the dominant culture. In short, it presupposes that a polity is possible only where its participants share a common culture. These assumptions have become particularly evident as the polities of the West have become subject to the strain of multicultural social conditions, and to a post-assimilationist politics of difference. As the very term "minorities" indicates, the dominant discourse of citizenship is still predicated on the idea of a common culture/civilization which, in order to be a citizen, individuals and groups must share. It bears emphasis that all official Australian citizenship discourse works in this way: when it refers to "special" groups, it indicates their status as outside the norm; when it uses the term "social justice," the word, "social" works as a qualifier in relation to what is taken to be the modal sort of justice.

III

I have argued, then, that the dominant discourses of modern citizenship are predicated on systemic exclusions of those who are othered by these discourses. These discourses cannot be corrected or reformed. This argument is now the more compelling because an alternative vision of citizenship, one that works with and accepts difference, is sufficiently emerged as to be named, if not yet theorized in a developed sense. In practical terms, this is the vision that we can find in Melbourne if we talk to advocates of multicultural service delivery. They do not introduce cultural/ethnic/lingual difference in order to develop more effective strategies of assimilation. They value this difference and design their services accordingly. Thus, it is not just that a service needs to be varied so that it is culturally appropriate for its potential range of culturally different users, but that in being so varied, the service will become altogether more dialogical, more responsive to the expressed needs of all the individuals using it. In short, it will become a service oriented to the substantive particularity of individual and group needs, where this orientation is a function of ongoing dialogue between users and service deliverers.

During the reform phases of the Hawke Government in Australia, roughly 1983–1987, there was some important experimentation, in policy and program terms, with making public services responsive to difference. Needs-based planning in child care, for example, was predicated on the idea of combining expert-supplied demographic information with qualitative information obtained through genuine consultation with what were assumed always as culturally different, potential users of a service. In relation to such consultation, the service assumed the features of an "emergent strategy," a service that would keep on developing and changing in relation to the expressed needs of the differentiated community for which it operates. To put it differently, in Joel Handler's (1988) terms, the decisions which inform the service are dialogical, negotiated, experimental and flexible.

There are now good theoretical elaborations of what it may mean to conceive citizenship in relation to a positive valuation of difference. Let me refer to just two.

Iris Marion Young's (1990b) work is oriented to rethinking justice and citizenship in relation to heterogeneous and differentiated communities. She begins with the premise that our societies are differentiated, especially in the sense that there are various axes of oppression which group people as either oppressed or dominant in respect of the particular axis concerned: race, ethnicity, gender, disability, age, sexuality, class. It is inevitable that these principles of social grouping work to generate distinct perspectives on what justice should look like, and how it might operate. Moreover, these differences in culture are not just a function of defensive adaptation to oppression. As oppressed groups have contested their oppression, they have re-valued, positively acclaimed, what it is that makes them different in relation to the dominant norm. In order to do this—to claim Black to be beautiful, for example—they have had to contest the norm itself, and to reconceptualize a *res publica* in a manner that makes it adequate to difference in a positive sense.

The starting point of these oppressed groups is the assumption of specificity of perspective: a Maori point of view, a Pakeha (see Note 1, Ch. 6) point of view. There is no privileged position of generality—no god's eye view. All then that is possible is for differently positioned groups or individuals to come together to offer their different perspectives on how they should decide and manage their shared life conditions. This is a perspectival dialogism, one which indicates that what justice is conceived to be is an historically moveable feast subject to the ongoing negotiation of these different perspectives and the provisional settlements they achieve. A pragmatic wisdom is thereby possible. The assumption is that these settlements will achieve a kind of wisdom, that they will stick for the time being, to the extent that they express a negotiated compromise between different perspectives.

There is an emerging literature which theorizes such a *civitas* oriented within a perspectival dialogism. For example, Andrew Sharp's (1990) *Justice and the Maori* shows how the Treaty of Waitangi has become treated as "fundamental law" in respect of the polity shared by Maori and Pakeha (see also McHugh, 1991). It has become so precisely because it has not been treated as a matter of reparative justice, as a point of reference for the restoration of rights breached by Pakeha in relation to Maori. Indeed, Sharp shows how the Tribunal which was set up to hear claims in relation to the Treaty of Waitangi has tended to avoid the clarity and unambiguities of contractual breach and rights talk. Instead, it has made decisions or, rather, recommendations which are oriented within a culture of prospective justice, that is, oriented in terms of what changes need to be made in order to conduce to a bicultural partnership. This is a partnership in which irresolvably different Maori and Pakeha conceptions of justice are to find voice, and in which a shared conception of justice must represent, not a rational consensus, but some kind of negotiated compromise in relation to these different conceptions of justice.

It is the spirit of the Treaty—its "principles"—rather than its letter which is taken to inform this fundamental law. This is precisely to afford the plasticity, the flexibility, and the discretion which permit and legitimize a future- rather than past-oriented shared process of negotiating the shape and content of the New Zealand polity. It is worth pointing out that all the qualities which Sharp finds in the discourse of the Treaty of Waitangi also obtain for what, as Joel Handler (1988) argues, should inform the culture of public services when the relationships concerned are ongoing (e.g. nursing home services). Handler makes the point precisely that the adversarial, rights-oriented culture of the law poorly serves when it is a matter of making such services more adequate to the expressed needs of their users. In particular, democratic service delivery requires there to be a high degree of discretion, in order to provide the space for what I call "a little polity" to develop between service deliverers and service users. Such a participatory approach to decisions permits a problem-solving approach to them. As Handler (1988, 1033) puts it: "By looking at the future in terms of multiple needs and objectives rather than hopelessly trying to reconstruct the past, parties have the opportunity to be creative."

It is important to appreciate that if an open, democratic politics of difference depends on the adoption of such a dialogical approach, this is a dialogical approach which works with and invites conflict and confrontation. The contestants have to extend each other enough good will and belief in the ongoing quality of their shared life conditions to cooperate in producing a provisional, negotiated settlement. However, what they decide to compromise on and accept as provisional principles of working together may as often arise out of listening to each other's point of contestation, conflict or simply difference in respect of the self's point of view.

I suggested above that a politics of difference requires the political community to be thought of in a post-ontological way. By this I mean, of course, that any empirical political community is bounded, and it has to be bounded in ways which establish insiders and outsiders. However, the way in which it understands this boundedness is critical. It can attribute boundedness to a pre-political, given community of being or make it a function of an historically contingent and contestable process of political community formation (for further elaboration of this distinction, see Chapter 6). While the former construction of the identity of the political community rules out a politics of difference, the latter does not.

It is clear that a democratic politics of difference requires this post-ontological type of political community to commit itself to certain kinds of proceduralism. If the contestants have to extend to each other enough good will and belief in the ongoing nature of their co-existence to make dialogue possible, this extension depends on their agreement to subordinate the bare assertion of their respective differences to some shared political norms. Such norms include the values of what Heller (1988) calls formal democracy as they include also a commitment to a universalistic orientation to the positive value of difference within a democratic political process. This is not simply liberal respect for the "difference" of the "minority" voice—the voice which is left out in the political settlement—but respect for the "differences" which are to inform the nature of those things which become *pro tem* and provisional political settlements.

There is much in the procedures required to foster a politics of difference which resembles new cultural techniques of managing change. The search technique (see Dick,1989), for example, in building a shared vision between all stakeholders in a particular context of decision-making, works with stakeholders' differences, and does not submerge or subsume them. The vision, therefore, has to be one which takes up the significance of these differences, builds them into where the organization or polity is going. This is the point behind resourcing self-identified cultures within a multicultural polity so that they can maintain and develop their own lingual and cultural sense of self.

The proceduralism which characterizes a polity oriented to difference is one which fosters more organic styles of decision-making than those of the legal-bureaucratic state which Weber theorizes. It is a proceduralism which positively values discretion in contexts where it can be assumed that there are dialogical means of making the discretion accountable. While this suggests that the system develops markedly decentralized qualities, decentralization has to be made accountable to policy guidelines that negotiated settlements for the polity as a whole have produced.

In order to include substantive features of selfhood, as well as substantive differences of positioning (in respect of both oppression and historical-cultural location), the procedural features and design of the above-mentioned system have to make a relative shift away from centralized, formal, rational-bureaucratic types of decision-making in the direction of context-responsive, organic and decentralized types of decision-making. While there has to be a macro-polity framing and guiding what happens within it, much of this system is better conceptualized as a series of interconnected polities, some local, some regional, some interregional, to use spatial metaphors. As for the macro-polity itself, its "givenness" is of an entirely historical, contingent variety, and subject to change, as the impact of supranational, political-legal, jurisdictional entities on nation-state jurisdictions would indicate.

A politics of difference cannot overcome the necessary dialectic of self and other. However, by situating selfhood in relation to a legitimate heterogeneity of perspectives, such a politics does not require the assertion of self to take the form of an essentialist positivity which not only others that which it is not, but forgets the necessary forgetting which accompanies the process of othering. Not only is the selfhood of the polity (of the civic culture) reconcilable with and dependent upon heterogeneity, but individual selves assume a flexibility and heterogeneity in this context. The individual no longer requires to be a natural essence of some kind, but can be oriented to him/herself as someone who has multiple, contradictory and historically changeful selves. In order to "be," the individual thereby has to adopt a negotiated, provisional-settlement approach to the production of his/her own acts and decisions. Among other things this means the individual as a political actor may assume a non-coherent, or a non-"party," identity. Indeed, the individual may practice different aspects of his/her selfhood in different kinds of political arena and struggle.

It follows that rights talk within the politics of difference will be different from the rights talk of natural law in liberal and republican discourse, where individuality is assumed to be a given in respect of the polity. The polity either respects or does not respect this individuality. In the politics of difference, rights are understood as dialectical and relational in respect of opening debate and discussion about how to positively alter relationships of oppression. They are dialogical rights, predicated fundamentally on a right to give voice and be listened to within the dialogical processes of decision-making. It can be seen that these rights are also distinct from those associated with welfare state citizenship in which the state makes a positive conferral of rights (e.g. the rights of women and children to enjoy protection from harmful assertion of natural individuality). As Handler and others have argued, positive rights of this kind are not easily claimed because their assertion depends on the expensive, difficult and adversarial system of legal process.

It is important to understand the deconstructive character of the relationship of the politics of difference to the established traditions of liberal and social democracy. The politics of difference calls into question the ways in which these traditions are unable to work positively with the value of difference. The primary contribution of the politics of difference is to politicize the nature and identity of the political community on which these traditions have depended. The identity and boundaries of the political community are now subject to politics in ways which both destabilize any appearance of a consensualist national tradition and bring to light the historically changeful artifice by which such traditions are constructed. At the same time, the politics of difference presupposes the achievements of liberal and social democracy in the very nature of its critique of them. Thus, if the politics of difference opens up a new kind of rights talk it is not to be understood as supplanting but as entering into relationship with the distinctive rights talk of both liberalism and social democracy, respectively.

What kinds of new understanding of liberal and social democracy may follow from this relationship is not yet clear. This is a project still to be undertaken. What is clear is that a civic culture of difference is predicated just as much as the modern cultures of citizenship on a *res publica* which is valued, developed and resourced. The abandonment of this idea by contemporary, market-oriented liberalism (an economic liberalism rather than a democratic liberalism) has gone unchecked in part because economic liberals have hijacked the positive valuation of difference and converted it into the assertion of market preference. They have made effective political capital out of a more-complex individuality's rejection of paternalistic-bureaucratic modes of operating public sector services, and have suggested market-oriented choice to be a more adequate vehicle for a self-determining and richly developed individuality. Niche marketing is the producer's response to individuality. Undoubtedly, both market choice and niche marketing are required for the postmodern individual to express his/her wants. However, choice and marketing cannot substitute for the public and political dialogic and performative processes through which this individual constitutes who he/she is in relation to others, what their shared and respective needs are and how they may best be met.

In totalizing the economy and thereby displacing the domain of public, political action, the new liberalism reasserts the principles of private property in ways which respond to and co-opt the politics of difference. Difference is homogenized within the category of consumer preference, and rendered a function of privately oriented and self-regarding action. The emergent theories of a citizenship oriented within the politics of difference represent a renewal of a publicly and politically oriented democratic discourse.

6

State and Community

What is the nature of the relationship between state and community? As we shall see, those key terms—state and community—mean quite different things depending on how the nature of community is conceived. To simplify matters, I am going to propose that, at present, we have to hand two quite different and opposed ideas of community and the state it informs.

The existence of a state is justified with reference to a community of interest that this state is designed to protect, regulate and advance. It is true that neo-classically trained economists tend to regard with considerable distaste the idea of this community of interest and its relationship to the state. They are trained to think in terms of individuals in rational pursuit of their private advantage, and have great difficulty in accepting the public ideals and virtues that are associated with the idea of a community of interest. Accordingly, they have difficulty granting the state much of a role in the conduct of our affairs. Where they grudgingly accept that there are some things privately-oriented rational individuals will not do—such as, for example, provide for the defense of the community or for those individuals whose needs cannot be met through market activity—they permit the state a severely restricted sphere of activity.

I am not going to defend the idea that there is a community of interest shared by individuals, a community that in the modern era is identified with the idea of being a national community. For my purposes it is enough to state that, the economists notwithstanding, most people believe that they are not only private-ly-oriented individuals, and that there are important values and life chances that they hold in common. Most people do not need persuasion that private, self-regarding orientations are not sufficient to provide the glue on which the trust that upholds the social bond depends. Nor do they need persuasion that there are many goods on which our life chances depend—goods like health, education, highways and waste disposal—that are provided both more adequately and effectively if they are approached as ventures shared and resourced in common.

If most people find the need for public values and public goods uncontestable, and in this sense give a ready assent to the idea that there is a community of interest which informs these public values and goods, this consensus breaks down when it becomes a matter of determining which or whose community of interest we may be talking about. The idea of the national community has become a thoroughly contested site of active political mobilization, where very different notions of this community of interest have become antagonists.

Since I am an Australian, let me offer an Australian example. In Australia at present two very different constructions of the Australian national community vie for presence on the state's policy agenda. The first invokes a nationalistic account of Australian identity where Australians are represented as sharing a common culture because they share common origins in their British roots. Here nationhood is understood in terms of the metaphors of kinship: it is common descent which underwrites the common culture on which national identity depends, and there is an elaborated narrative of sons and daughters who left a "mother country" to establish a new settler colony. The second invokes the idea of a particular set of conventional, national institutions which have their own distinctive ethic and history, and which are still evolving in ways which permit the society they constitute to become adequate to the present challenges of feminism, postcolonialism and multiculturalism. The national community on this account becomes one which is oriented internally to issues of access and equity for, especially, women, non-English-speaking-background Australians and Aboriginal Australians. Externally, this national community is oriented to finding a place of respect and integrity within the predominantly Asian regional community of its nearest neighbors.

Necessarily, the proponents of the first construction of the Australian national community are offended and outraged by the ideas of a multicultural Australia which is officially seeking to become regarded as an Asian nation. There are parallel debates within New Zealand. In New Zealand, leaving aside the resistance of white settler nationalism to claims on national justice by the indigenous colonized, it is clear that biculturalism can be understood in terms of either of these two general accounts of the national community. On the first account, biculturalism is understood to be both a process and an outcome which foregrounds issues of how two separate and distinct peoples (or communities of descent) are to pursue their lives within the same territorial state jurisdiction. This version of biculturalism places it in a mutually exclusive relationship to multiculturalism. On the second account, biculturalism is understood to be a process and outcome whereby Maori and Pakeha are each culturally and socially resourced in ways which permit them an empowered and effective relationship to ongoing dialogue as to how to shape the social and civic life which they are committed to sharing.[1] When biculturalism is approached as a dialogical matter concerning non-exclusive cultural identities, not only can Maori and Pakeha explore their influence on and kinship with each other, but this version of biculturalism can be positively linked to multicultural values and objectives.

We can term these two different approaches to and accounts of a national community the customary and conventionalist accounts, respectively. They offer quite distinct and opposing grounds for why a national community comes into existence in the first place and how it is maintained over time. In other words, they throw up entirely different kinds of politics which, in turn, generate entirely different kinds of policy approaches to public values and public goods. Let me elaborate.

The polity which is based in a customary nationalism is one which is regulated by the ideal of a customary national community. As I proposed, this customary national community is structured in terms of the logic of kinship. This accords it two primary axes: vertically, the axis of descent, or the relationship between progenitors and their progeny; and, horizontally, the axis of a procreatively-oriented distinction between male and female. All who come under the nation are understood to be its children because they share in a community of descent. Their shared status as children, however, is differentiated in terms of gender. The sovereign state is accorded the masculine role of protecting the motherland or mother-country. Men become brothers in their duty of sacrifice on behalf of military defense of the motherland. Thus, Benedict Anderson (1991, 7, emphasis in the original), in his influential work on nation-states as imagined communities, proposes that the state "is imagined as a *community*, because, regardless of the actual inequality and exploitation that may prevail in each, the nation is always conceived as a deep, horizontal comradeship." He proceeds: "Ultimately it is this fraternity that makes possible, over the past two centuries, for so many millions of people, not so much to kill, as willingly to die for such limited imaginings." (See also Elshtain, 1991.) Women's duty is archetypally that of the mothers who have reared the male citizens whose lives may be sacrificed for national honor. National honor is identified with the integrity of this community of descent and the territory with which it is associated.

The existence of this national community depends on its exclusiveness. It is this, not that national community of common descent. While intermarriage and shared histories which intimately link this national community to its immediate neighbors are acknowledged in everyday life, these interconnections are denied within the national imaginary for they clearly challenge the idea of this community as a separate and exclusive one. This is a national community whose sense of self demands it go to war if these exclusive boundaries of community and territory are threatened by another national community.

We have only to recall what has happened in the former Yugoslavia to grasp how deep is the hold the customary ideal of a national community still exercises. It is this ideal which upheld the welfare state that was instituted in state societies like New Zealand, Australia and Britain in the period of the 1930's and 1940's. If the core institutions of the welfare state are examined, it becomes clear that they are structured by these vertical and horizontal axes of the customary national community. Thus, welfare entitlements are structured in terms of the kinship status of their claimants. In particular, from the point of view of labor market policy and welfare, married women are presumed to be determined by their role as mothers, a role which should be economically supported by a husband's family wage, or, where this is lacking, by a state pension.

The polity which is upheld by the conventionalist account of national community is not structured in terms of the metaphors and idiom of kinship. It is upheld instead by a legal-conventionalist view of how it is that its members come together and of what legally-sanctioned values they must have in common. Immigration law and policy make explicit the understandings which are left implicit in how those born within this national community are educated and trained as its members. State policy as both legislation and administrative guidelines produce a world regulated by some basic common values. Since these values cannot ground trust and mutual respect in kinship idiom, they have to appeal to the universalistic non-kinship idiom of justice. This is an idiom which is elaborated in terms of values like equal opportunity, anti-discrimination, equity, equality, due process, natural justice, individual rights to participation, and the like.

Here the national community is understood to be one that is constructed in terms of the historically specific traditions and conventions of a particular national democracy. These traditions and conventions are understood to be contestable in terms of the value of political participation by all those who belong to this national community. This community is one which has to have clear legal-juridical boundaries, which determine who belongs and who does not, but it does not depend on the idea of being based in mutually exclusive kinship community. Accordingly, it has no difficulty in understanding that its politics must and will reflect an internal politics of difference in respect of ethnic-lingual community. This internal politics of difference is linked into the way that this national community understands its external ties and challenges. If there is a substantial number of first-generation Australians with ties to Vietnam, Hong Kong, Singapore and Malaysia, this must affect how Australia's immigration policy is directed. It affects specifically how many immigrants from these countries are accepted into Australia by increasing their presence both within the family reunion and skill-tested components of the immigration program.

This type of national community necessarily calls into question customary, or culturally exclusive kinship-ethnic loyalties. Its own multicultural commitments require it to provide public resources to maintain the cultural integrity of its participant ethnic groups. Thus, for example, the Australian state has funded ethno-specific child care services. However, paradoxically enough, cultural integrity is to be understood in a non-exclusive fashion. Thus, if non-Polish parents want to send their children to a Polish child-care center in Adelaide, the state requires the center to accept them. In short, the center is to be genuinely and practically bicultural and bilingual, working with both mainstream and specific cultural identities for all the children and their parents using it. This is an entirely different understanding from that which prevails when "biculturalism" is taken to mean an exclusively Polish language and culture child care center. It is a "biculturalism" which is oriented to working positively with the values of cultural difference and diversity. In this it can be seen to promote multiculturalism, and a more generalized value of what might be termed cultural "flexibility."

Non-exclusive cultural identity formation is a social project which invites exploration of hyphenated and multiple identities. There is no requirement of individuals that they be one cultural identity or another. They can be both, Polish-Australian for example, or in the New Zealand setting, Maori and Pakeha. It is also a social project which accepts that within any one particular cultural group there will be multiple and contested views as to the nature of that group's identity and the ways it should be expressed. Accordingly, if, in a society such as Australia, where over 20 per cent of the total population are of non-English-speaking background, different ethnic communities must be consulted so as to make services culturally responsive, these consultations occur with a range of representatives of these groups, not just their official spokes*men*.

At present, conventionalist understandings of national community have very shallow roots. They are only lightly anchored in the soil of existing nations. It is arguable they have no intergenerational depth beyond what may be happening in the imaginations of those who have come to political maturity in the postwar postcolonial era. They throw up new tasks for the state and the business of governance, and, as I wish to emphasize below, they require the business of governance to be more democratically accountable than has occurred in the past.

II

First, however, let us return to what I have termed the customary national community and the kind of state it authorizes. It is important to explain why I have termed this national community a customary one.

As Benedict Anderson (1991) argues, it is one of the paradoxes of nationalism that it refers to a way of imagining the world that is of relatively recent origins, but that each national imaginary tells a story of the ancient or primordial origins of the national community concerned. Even where this is difficult to sustain, as in the case of white settler colonies such as the United States, Canada, Australia or New Zealand (a problem to which I shall return), the national imaginary invokes the national origins of these settlers as the cultural foundation stones of the new nation. In other cases, such as the relatively new nations of Iran or Indonesia, there is a retroactive reading of national origins which links the new nation to peoples of antiquity or of the pre-colonial era. Thus, the Shah of Iran linked his nation back to the ancient Persian empire; and "the late President

Sukarno always spoke with complete sincerity of the 350 years of colonialism that his 'Indonesia' had endured, although the very concept 'Indonesia' is a twentieth-century invention, and most of today's Indonesia was only conquered by the Dutch between 1850 and 1910". (Anderson, 1991, 11, note 4).

A customary national community works in terms of the idea that the community already exists in an unproblematic way. It is a "natural" community, where "natural" here connotes what are taken to be the organic, customary ties of communities built on common descent and customarily shared ways of life. Aristotle's construction of the *polis* is an example of this kind of thinking. The polis is constructed of the building blocks of first, procreative couples and their households of children and slaves, second, the villages which are made up of these households, and, third, the city-state which is made up of a number of these villages.

It follows that the role of the state is to *recognize* rather than to *constitute* the national community. In this sense the life and ways of the national community are accorded a pre-political status. They are not legitimately subject to open political contestation and debate. Of course, we know that all tradition is constantly reinvented (see Hobsbawm and Ranger, 1983), but this invention proceeds in terms of the uncontested authority of the original source. Thus, interpretations of the original vary over time, but these variations are masked by being made to appear authoritative readings of the original. For example, the customary narrative of the free-born Englishman is one which is invoked by a wide range of political actors from Shakespeare's Henry V to nineteenth-century Chartists to Churchill. That well-known call to battle of Shakespeare's Henry V illustrates perfectly this idea of a customary national community:

> ...And you, good yeomen,
> Whose limbs were made in England, show us here
> The mettle of your pasture; let us swear
> That you are worth your breeding: which I doubt not;
> For there is none of you so mean and base,
> That hath not lustre in your eyes.
> I see you stand like greyhounds in the slips,
> Straining upon the start. The game's afoot:
> Follow your spirit; and upon this charge
> Cry—God for Harry! England! and Saint George!

Act III, Scene 1, lines 25–34

A customary national community declares itself in such invocation of God and of canonized ancestral figures like Saint George. What Nietzsche (1982) calls the "sense of custom" is expressed in the way that the state and public policy operate when they are informed by this kind of national community. There are two broad aspects of this operation to which I wish to draw attention. First, this is a state which operates in terms of the patriarchal paternalism of this type of national community. Accordingly, the orientation of the state to the members of the national community is one of paternalistic *protection*. Democracy in this state is of a particular kind. It is oriented to what Carole Pateman (1988) calls the "fratriarchy" of individual male patriarchs or heads of households. These male patriarchs are accorded recognition as heads of households by the state, and it is assumed that they will appropriately express the culture of patriarchal protection within these households. This means that the majority of people in this society as well as huge areas of social life are left within the pre-political or private domain of individual patriarchal discretion. This, then, is a non-interventionist state as far as both the lives of women and children, and the social business of caring, are concerned. It is also a non-interventionist state in respect of what are taken to be the legitimate prerogatives of private property within the relationships of economic production.

From the standpoint of the values of democratic participation, this is a rather primitive kind of state. This is underlined in its second aspect, namely its tendency to be oriented by the morality of custom. People are expected to obey the ways of this national community, not to subject them to critical and reflective scrutiny. Political action tends to be expressed as politically correct, ritual profession of these ways. Instead of subjecting an orientation and course of action to rational determination of how the cause and effect relationship may operate in this instance, the actors in this community of custom believe it necessary only to state their (it goes without saying) good intentions. If it should turn out that the consequences of their action fall somewhat short of their proclaimed intention that is not their responsibility. As Nietzsche (1982, 14) savagely put it, in this morality consequence is thought of "as supplement":

> Formerly people believed that the outcome of an action was not a consequence but a free supplement—namely God's. Is a greater confusion conceivable? The action and its outcome had to be worked at separately, with quite different means and practices!

A customary morality cannot make for either a sophisticated or responsible culture of public policy. Such a policy is attuned to the difficulties of a calculus of means, ends and unintended consequences. It operates in terms of what Max Weber (1970) termed an "ethic of responsibility." Weber, himself a student of Nietzsche, contrasted what he called an "ethic of ultimate ends" with this ethic of responsibility. An ethic of ultimate ends operates when political actors proclaim an absolute adherence to a particular value, and leave the consequences to take care of themselves. As Weber was at pains to point out, an ethic of responsibility is a much more prosaic and pragmatic business than the heroics of an ethic of ultimate ends.

It is clear that a customary morality, in declaring off limits a reflexive means–ends–unintended consequences calculus, makes for considerable rigidity in potential public policy responses to contemporary problems and challenges. A conventionalist subscription to such a reflexive calculus, on the other hand, opens up considerable flexibility in these responses.

An ethic of ultimate ends fits, however, the exclusive and separatist ethos of a customary national community. We can consider the invocations of the free market by politicians such as Ronald Reagan and Margaret Thatcher. Are these new twists on the customary morality of "the land of the free," on the one hand, and "free-born Englishmen" on the other? Certainly these invocations work in terms of the sense of custom, not the sense of rational reflection on means-ends-consequences relationships. Their expression is in terms of a politically correct flying of customary national symbols, not in terms of a democratic invitation to the nation's citizens to thoughtfully participate in the currently challenging business of economic restructuring.

The culture of public policy which fits this type of state is restricted within the customary ethos of paternalistic protection. It does not favor or promote any of the conditions for political participation: freedom of information, advocacy services for the more vulnerable groups (those for whom paternalistic protection turns out to be paternalistic abuse), and publicly-funded resources for public learning, such as national electronic media, which have a brief to educate the citizenry in a critical culture of rational policy discussion and debate.

To conclude these remarks on the customary national community and the kind of state to which it gives rise, it is clear that this type of state has increasingly lost legitimacy over the last thirty or so years. It has faced two concerted challenges. The first has come from feminism, which has contested the patriarchal paternalism of this kind of customary nation-state. Feminists find it difficult to accept the traditions of national heroism associated with this state, authorizing as such traditions do these words of Shakespeare's King Harry before the Gates of Harfleur:

> If I begin the battery again,
> I will not leave the half-achieved Harfleur
> Till in her ashes she lie buried.
> The gates of mercy shall be all shut up;
> And the flesh'd soldier,—rough and hard of heart,—
> In liberty of bloody hand shall range
> With conscience wide as hell; mowing like grass
> Your fresh-fair virgins and your flowering infants.

Act III, Scene 2, lines 7–14

If feminists open up the customary privacy of patriarchal households to the policy attention of the state, the various postcolonial antiracist and multicultural movements contest the customary nation-state's cultural exclusivism. They point out that this state has only two options with regard to those it conquers: assimilation, the absorption of the barbarian; or genocide. While feminists contest a national community structured in terms of a paternalism which ensures that women and children are non-citizens, these postcolonial movements require this national community to be constructed in terms of a non-exclusive and complex cultural identity. This cultural complexity has to be one which invites the self-identified different cultural groups living within the one nation state to explore the terms of their co-existence in ways which challenge the *customary* dominance of the mainstream lingual-cultural group. This dominance has now to become accountable to and transformed by the conventionalist values of equality of opportunity, anti-discrimination, culturally-appropriate service design and delivery, and rights of individual participation in service design and delivery.

As Andrew Sharp (1992) has recently pointed out, the adherents of the customary national community ideal do not relinquish it just because it becomes contested. Indeed not, since this is an ideal structured in terms of the ethic of ultimate ends. It is not an ideal responsive to pragmatic or empirical considerations. This is as true of colonizing customary nationalism as it is of the customary nationalism of the colonized. Among other things, this means that we are making a signal mistake if we arraign customary and conventionalist nationalisms as, respectively, two progressive steps on an evolutionary social ladder. What we need to explore and interrogate is the simultaneity, the co-sequential existence of these two very different narratives of the bases of national community. Conventionalism may turn out to be the product of a deconstructive and critical re-working of customary nationalism.

III

Let me say something more of what I have termed the conventionalist national community. This is a national community which understands its ethos and integrity to lie in its distinctive political history of making itself into an independent nation-state, where "independence" connotes a self-determining political community of participating citizens. This project of making itself refers not to the origins of this state but to the process through which it becomes whatever particular state it is at present. This orientation to processes of self-fabrication as a particular nation-state community is what underwrites the conventionalism of its political culture.

This is a political culture which puts a premium on policy discussion and debate because it is assumed that this state cannot know what it is, or where it should go, without rational scrutiny of who comprises it and where it has come from. Contrary to the customary nation-state, this political culture is preeminently pragmatically and empirically minded. If the population is aging, or

AIDS has become a problem, the policy response is threefold: 1. commission the academic researchers to chart the empirical dimensions of the problem; 2. draw those who will work with the problem both as sufferers and service deliverers into the brainstorming and problem-solving that is to inform the policy response; and 3. get the policy-makers (state bureaucrats and politicians) to design a policy on the basis of all this information. This policy response is understood not as absolute but as an emergent strategy of political management of what will be ongoing developments in both the nature of the problem and the learning about it.

This is a political culture which is oriented to the promotion of processes of public learning and participation. It is assumed that it is impossible to do anything sensible about the challenges which face the national community unless all of its members are drawn into discussion about the nature of these challenges and how best to respond to them. This assumption operates because there is a non-paternalistic and democratic culture of participation within this national community.

This, of course, is the interventionist state which has aroused the ire of those champions of the customary national community: Maggie Thatcher and Ronald Reagan. Precisely because this state works with consequences, it brings to surface the tricky pragmatics of working with complex means-ends-consequences relationships. This is a state which tends to name all aspects of social life, to bring them out of customary morality and to subject them to some kind of rational *and* participatory calculus. It thereby invites as it legitimizes debate about what the problems are and how they should be responded to. Experience in this policy culture of the conventionalist state acquaints its participants with all the complexities of value trade-offs and dilemmas. This is a world where the participants attempt to provide sensible and provisional policy responses in the light of what appear to be the most relevant values and information.

It is a decidedly non-heroic political culture. Pragmatic compromise and incremental reform tend to be the hallmarks of this culture, rather than the absolutism of either conservative patriarchalism or its revolutionary counterparts.

IV

Can we find instances of conventionalist national communities which foster this kind of state-centric culture of public policy? I would argue that we can, albeit instances which are historically recent and which have been permitted little maturation.

Let me take the Australian case again, it being the one I know best. First, it is worth remark that Australia, like the United States, Canada and New Zealand, belongs to the "New World." While these nation-states explicitly claim to be offshoots of a customary and primordial national community, as politically independent states they are forced to "stand on their own feet" and establish their own charters of existence. Precisely because they have an origin which they cannot use to ground this charter—they are not English colonies any more—they have to adopt the metaphor of self-fabrication. It is not ancient custom but modern democratic values which legitimize these states.

Democratic values have changed over the course of the modern epoch. In the seventeenth century, as understood by Hobbes and Locke, democratic values meant that individual patriarchal householders or owners of private property entered into a social contract to establish a state which would regulate and protect this national community of individual property owners. Protection of private property not only left the customary patriarchal authority of householders intact but it licensed the separation of indigenous peoples from their land because it was argued they were not usefully cultivating this land. The United States is a New World state society formed in terms of the ethos of these patriarchalist democratic values. Its War of Independence and founding Constitution were in the name of the democratic theories associated with Locke and Montesquieu.

Both Australia and New Zealand were colonial state formations until the latter half of the nineteenth century. Australia's founding principles mixed the ignominy of a convict settlement with the civic virtues of a Wakefield scheme for an independent land-holding yeomanry in South Australia. From the beginning, this mixed a highly state-centric culture of administrative direction with the principles of private property.

Australia's independence has never been too secure, since its status as a formally independent satellite of the North-Atlantic, US-led metropolis in the postwar era has been expressed in its ongoing hospitality to US military bases and Prime Minister Harold Holt's infamous words during the Vietnam War, "All the way with LBJ." It has been the political contestation of this satellite status mixed with the contemporary significance of multicultural and feminist movements that has brought the Australian state into a postcolonial mode. It is this which explains the hegemony of Labor in the leadership of the Australian state in the period 1973 to the present. Labor was the party which was best able to respond to the mix of urbanism, ethnic complexity, feminism and the Australianization of intellectual life and higher education which have characterized the Australian society of the 1970's and 1980's.

Over this period, Labor Governments have fostered a policy-oriented conventionalist state and national community. Several examples of this may be given from the period of the early 1980's to the early 1990's. The national AIDS policy in Australia from its inception involved gay and prostitute organizations in its design and delivery. The development of an official National Multicultural Agenda meant a nationally coordinated effort by both Commonwealth and State and Territory Governments to do something effective about the recognition of overseas qualifications. Thirdly, for a complex of reasons having to do with Labor's tripartite corporatist approach and an overall commitment to access and equity, there has been from 1988 to now (1993) an extraordinary, national, systemic effort to coordinate the restructuring of national industrial awards, the development of a competency approach to all occupations including the professions, and the restructuring of higher education and technical training. This is fostering enormous sophistication of awareness and involvement among all the constituencies involved.

Australia now is more like a conventionalist national community than it is like a customary one. However, like all modern state formations this community is susceptible to the legitimacy of a modern version of a customary principle. I refer to the ongoing legitimacy of patriarchal private property. Locke and the other early modern democratic theorists grounded the right of private property in a right of "nature." It was thus an inalienable, a God-given right. Indeed, it was because God had created free and independent individual patriarchal householders that the conventionalist approach to state formation became necessary. Hence the account of the state in terms of a social contract between these individual householders. As Rousseau (1968) insisted, we need to examine how it is a people becomes a people. Here a conventionalist and a customary account come together. God or nature represent the origins of what has to become by human artifice a conventional state, but the extent and sphere of this state's legitimacy is bounded by its role in protecting customary or natural property right.

White settler dispossession of the land from the Aboriginal or indigenous peoples of North America, Australia and New Zealand was undertaken in the name of natural property right. This was a private or individualized property right which could not accommodate the claims of tribal or collective property right (see Fleras and Elliott, 1992, especially Ch.10). Thus, the assertion of the natural right of settlers against the indigenous, first occupants of the land generated a customary national community and its institutions which expressed white settler natural right.

Private property can be justified in terms of natural right (the customary defense) or in terms of convention. If the former, then the state simply recognizes and does not interfere with property right. If the latter, the state actually institutes property right. What follows from this is an economy which mixes the principles of state intervention and conventional private property right. It is important to understand that the idea of a mixed economy cannot become a mature idea until a conventionalist approach to state and community has become an established approach. Neither Marxism nor organized Labor have been able to relinquish the patriarchal ideal of natural right, namely the ideal of individual householder private property as the Marxist conception of alienation and Labor's historic attachment to the family wage respectively bear out. It is arguable, then, that one of the tasks of the present is to develop a conventionalist approach to private property, including those forms which are tribal in character.

V

To return to my beginning, I suggested that most of us have no trouble accepting that there is such a thing as a community of interest which it is the business of the state to promote, regulate and defend. I have argued, however, that under feminist, multicultural and postcolonial challenges, there has developed serious disagreement as to the bases of this community of interest. I have suggested that this disagreement concerns whether these bases are customary ("natural") or conventional in character. These two different approaches generate quite different kinds of state and quite different approaches to public policy.

I have suggested that the customary approach faces an ongoing crisis of legitimacy in the face of feminist, multicultural and postcolonial challenges, a crisis for which the conventionalist approach is much better equipped. I have shifted my focus to the New World where customary accounts of national community as a community of descent are more difficult to sustain in the light of the postcolonial break with the "mother country." However, conventionalism as an approach to state and community in these contexts is opposed not so much by customary forms of nationalism as it is by defenses of private property which argue private property as a matter of custom (natural right) rather than convention. Here, then, it is a customary market principle which ensures conventionalism is a minority and critical approach.

If Australian state society under the national leadership of Labor 1973–1975 and 1983 to the present offers an interesting example of the potential of a conventionalist approach to contemporary issues, its exemplary status may extend no further than itself. For each state society is its own distinctive historical creature inheriting a particular set of contradictions concerning these two different approaches to national identity and state action.

Moreover, the internationalization of national economies has posed new demands, calling for conventionalist approaches to economic activity. In the face of this internationalization, which is undermining all the established institutions of a national mixed economy, it is all too easy for the proponents of a customary or absolute private property right to have it all their way. A conventionalist reassertion of the principles of a mixed economy needs to understand how to institutionally respond to internationalization. This will take some time. Whatever else, an effective capacity to respond in this way will depend on an ability to work with non-exclusive cultural identity since our economies and their entanglements are increasingly cross-cultural in character.

Until there is a newly relevant defense of the principles of the mixed economy, we can expect the idea of the welfare state to be in some disarray. As I have suggested, the established welfare state ideal was tied to an ideal of national community which could not withstand contemporary feminist, multicultural and postcolonial challenge. Again, this has provided a vacuum which the proponents of natural private property right have been only too ready to fill.

I have emphasized conventionalist approaches to state and community as unheroic, pragmatic and reformist. They tend to call into question culturally exclusive accounts of community and the kinds of undemocratic practice such exclusion justifies. By undermining culturally exclusive accounts of community identity, conventionalist approaches to state and community call into question the ethic of ultimate ends which follows on cultural exclusivity. The end must always justify the means in a culturally exclusive defense of identity which refuses to acknowledge the way in which identity (of communities and individuals) is never pure and always mixed. Conventionalism, on the other hand, encourages an ethic of responsibility in which attention is paid to the complexity of means-ends-consequence relationships. On this ethic it is understood that good intentions are no guarantee of outcomes.

Conventionalist approaches to state and community require a renewal of democratic values in which these are informed by non-exclusive accounts of cultural identity. Such a renewal has to be guided by an acceptance of the cultural complexity of the community on which the state depends, an acceptance which is upheld by regulative values like anti-discrimination, affirmative action and equal opportunity. These values depend on an active culture of non-paternalistic state intervention which is expressed in a mixed economy relevant to the needs of the present.

7
Postmodernity and Revisioning the Political

I

There is no reason, only reasons.
—Jean-François Lyotard in Van Riejen and Veerman, *An Interview with Jean-François Lyotard*, 1988

Postmodernity is the condition we are in now, a condition under which there is no operative consensus concerning the ultimate or transcendental grounds of truth and justice. This is why Lyotard (1984) identifies the postmodern condition with a crisis of narratives, or more specifically, of meta-narratives, stories which ground truth and justice in some kind of metaphysical presence such as Reason, Nature or God.

Where there can be no consensus derived from a shared culture of orientation to such transcendental grounds, the consequence for truth and justice is simple. Some other approach than that of basing them in shared transcendental grounds has to be found. If this approach is consensualist in the sense of requiring agreement on how to approach decisions concerning truth and justice, there is no guarantee that this agreement is anything more than a highly provisional and pragmatic adaptation to the conditions of contestation over these values, and how they are to be interpreted.

Here I want to discuss the kind of politics that such provisional and pragmatic adaptation involves. Because it is politics rather than knowledge that is of concern, truth enters the picture only as it is one of the criteria in relation to which the legitimacy of claims on political process are assessed and judged. For example, in the politics of needs formation in an area such as home and community care for people who are disabled seriously enough to need help in the tasks of everyday living, there are patterned disagreements between how these individuals judge their needs, and how their needs are judged by the professionals involved (gerontologists, specialists in palliative care, physiotherapists and so on).[1]

The professionals deal in the business of what they like to think are real or objective needs, that is, needs as assessed in accordance with the knowledge base of the profession concerned. The disabled individuals think of these needs as their own, as taking on shape and existence through the way that they give voice to them: they are their expressed needs. Moreover, they accord themselves a special kind of expertise with regard to these needs: who can know them better than the person experiencing the needs? Then there are the informal carers, that is, spouses, close kin and sometimes friends who provide personally-oriented, regular assistance to the disabled individuals with whom they are connected. They have a carer's construction of the disabled individual's needs: a construction which is that of a close, personally involved observer, whose own needs are implicated in how the burden of meeting this individual's needs is distributed. The perspectives of the professional service deliverer, the carer and the needy person on the latter's needs and how they might best be met are irreducibly multiple, and often conflict.

One can make a policy decision, as the Commonwealth Government of Australia has done, to make the principle of determining how an individual's need is to be provided for one of responding to the expressed needs of the individual. This principle operates as a guideline in respect of determining how to weight these various judgments as to what the need is, and, correlatively, how it might be best met. Such a principle does not, however, resolve the ongoing tensions between the different perspectives on need. All it does and can do is to provide a principle of regulation of what I call the politics of needs formation.

This example is a good one for other reasons as well. The Commonwealth Government's policy of guiding services to work with the expressed needs of individuals in the home and community care area is in line with the general emphasis of the relevant bureaucratic department (the Department of Health, Housing and Community Services) on user rights. This, in turn, is in line with contemporaneous expectations of democratic service delivery: there have been a number of social movements contesting professional domination in needs formation, not least of these being the disabled people's movements of the 1970's and 1980's. These expectations have destabilized the welfare state culture of needs definition in which expert professional opinion guided the way that policy-makers framed needs and the services responding to those needs. This was a centric culture of scientifically informed needs formation which preempted an open politics of needs formation in favor of professional expertise. It is a political culture which favors the rhetoric of rational consensus. Once there is an open and legitimate difference of perspectives on needs formation the rhetoric of rational consensus is no longer operable. It is supplanted by a rhetoric of negotiated needs settlement where the principle of user rights provides guidance toward achievement of an effective and practical compromise between these perspectives. Each perspective is necessary because it provides a basic piece of information about the context which informs the needs concerned.

For example, with dementia sufferers, it is critical that the most up-to-date medical and scientific information about dementia is known by the relevant policy-makers in their construction of, not only the field of services required to care for people with dementia, but of these needs themselves. At the same time, the demographic profile of carers, the stress experienced by the carers of people with dementia, and their range of supports, are all relevant pieces of information to determining what needs will require formal service provision. At the moment, the Commonwealth Government funds ADARDS, which is an organization which both resources carer support (self-help) groups, and articulates/advocates the needs of both dementia sufferers and their carers to the relevant government agencies and service delivery organizations. Finally, while people suffering dementia are not usually in a position to assert their needs as user rights, Commonwealth Government policy is oriented to the development of advocacy services which will make this assertion on their behalf.

Anyone who knows the areas of needs formation and service provision to which I am referring knows that they are highly politicized environments in which the actors are becoming increasingly politically mature. There is no easy acceptance of this politics from the professionals at this stage: they hang onto the older culture of needs formation within which their expertise was accorded a virtual monopoly in the representation of needs to governments. At the same time, both the needy individuals and their carers are, many of them, highly dissatisfied with what are scarce and rationed services. These are not just highly politicized environments: they are also fraught. Needs settlements pass in and out of phases of negotiation and confrontation. Often confrontation is between advocates of user/carer rights, on the one hand, and professionals who resist this principle as one which undermines their own authority. There is an historicity to this field of political force which arises out of the way that needy individuals have appropriated the collectivist imaginary of self-determination and applied it to the field of human services provision. The current resistance of professionals is likely to give way over time, and, with the next generation of professionals, become a more accommodating and more subtle assertion of professional-knows-best.

The value of this example is also to underline how "the" polity has lost a clearly bounded centricity. It has become a more or less (dis)continuous series of polities. These polities are not given but struggled for: they arise out of what Alberto Melucci (1988, 258–260) calls the opening of "public spaces." This particular example of a polity involves the interpenetration of the state and everyday life in respect of areas of individual need usually reserved for what we would term personal privacy (e.g. the activities of an individual being washed, fed, toileted, and so on). It is an example which is outside the scope of the classical liberal and republican democratic polity of modernity. In this polity, needs of the kind to which I am referring were left to the private and natural business of the internal life of households. They were ministered to by those whose life was contained within the private world of the household (wives, mothers, daughters and servants). These non-citizens permitted the citizens, the heads of households, to represent the business of the polity as both quite separate from these private needs, and as much more important than them. Theirs was a unicity of rationalist hubris and public prestige, stable as long as their own status as masters of their own culture and independent property owners remained unthreatened.

A number of left, masculinist commentators (Lasch, Leach, and Donzelot) have pointed out that it was the professionals who laid the foundations of the welfare state and who undermined the integrity of this classical picture of a neat division between things public and things private. Male doctors who were licensed by the state toward the end of the nineteenth century, and who began to legitimize the intervention of the state into private lives in the areas of public and maternal/infant health, embarked on a treacherous alliance with, especially, middle-class mothers to undermine the patriarchal privilege of heads of households. The development of a universal, compulsory public school system worked in the same direction. However, the compromise between property rights and social rights which the welfare state represented maintained a principle of patriarchal determination of needs. This time it was expressed on behalf of a corporate representation of households—the state— and, in due measure, involved a transfer of rights from individual heads of households to the state in respect of the members of households. Corporate patriarchalism functioned thus to emancipate those who had been subject to the individual patriarchal householder's will. This is why interventionist doctors found ready allies amongst many, though largely amongst middle-class, women. It is also why such *fin-de-siècle* social scientists as Emile Durkheim, committed to the path of rational social reform, argued for a positive theory of right against the doctrine of natural right (see Chapter Six). Durkheim—in his lectures published as *Professional Ethics and Civic Morals*—argued that these clear instances of the state bestowing rights on individuals showed that right is always a matter of positive law. Natural right, which seems to indicate that law merely reflects rather than creates the rights of individuals, is a doctrine that does not accord with the facts. Durkheim offers a benign view of the modern interventionist state, one uncomplicated by late-twentieth-century awareness that the positive constitution of rights by the state comes at the expense of the bureaucratization of the spheres in which they operate.

At the same time, this construction of the polity in the form of the welfare state is considerably more relevant than the older liberal/republican democratic construction of the polity. Where the latter offers a very simple picture of the business of governance as essentially no more than the making and enforcement of law, the former shows how the interventionist state makes the executive and administrative aspects of governance just as central to the life of the polity as the legislative aspects. This begins to complicate the principle of representative government: the legislature may be representative, but to what extent is this true of the executive, let alone of the large and complex organizations that the administration of the state has come to involve? Moreover, an interventionist state politicizes by naming hitherto nonpolitical areas of social life and drawing them within the ambit of policy (see Yeatman, 1990b, chapter 8). The increasing reach of policy both deprivatizes and denatures aspects of social life hitherto regulated within the local patriarchal and customary communities of families, firms and service provision. In so doing, policy constitutes all who come within its reach as potential political actors who can open this area to a politics of voice and representation.

As we have seen with the example of the area of home and community care, a politics of voice and representation introduces the principle of irresolvable difference into the way that political process and decisions operate. This principle destabilizes and delegitimizes the paternalism of the state which it had borrowed from the patriarchal, paternalist authority of private households. This means that paternalism is no longer adequate to the vertical integration functions of social and political control at a time when the state is subject to an historically unparalleled politics of voice and representation. For paternalism, the state substitutes performativity as the principle which legitimizes both its control functions, and the way in which those functions operate to contain the influence of the horizontally integrated, democratic politics of social movements and their claims on the state. The state is thereby subject to the contradictory dynamics of performativity and democratization. Performativity has the singular virtue of supplying a meta-discourse for public policy. Thus it can subsume and transform substantive democratizing claims within a managerialist-functionalist rhetoric. Performativity is a systems-orientation: instead of the state appearing as the enlightened and paternal command of shared community, the state is equated with the requirements of a system for ongoing integrity and viability. This is a cybernetic model: "The true goal of the system, the reason it programs itself like a computer, is the optimization of the global relationship between input and output—in other words, performativity" (Lyotard, 1984, 11).

II

The decision makers...allocate our lives for the growth of power.
—Jean-François Lyotard, *The Postmodern Condition,* 1984

Performativity as a principle of governance depends on the existence of jurisdictional boundaries of the state which permit it to be thought of as a discrete system. However, the very nature of the cybernetic metaphor makes these boundaries open to input and output flows of information, capital and population within which the regulative presence of the boundaries operates like a program in relation to these flows, and where the limits of the program are set, reviewed and revised in state policy decisions. Performativity is a principle of governance which establishes strictly functional relations between a state and its inside and outside environments. Democracy and social welfare are operationalized in terms of these functional relations. The rhetoric of the state addressed to its own internal population takes on the features of an instrumentally rational orientation to the terms of economic competition between states and/or states allied together in trading blocks: Cerny (1990, chapter 8) refers to this development as a shift from the welfare to the competition state: Cerny (1990, 230) argues that: "As the world economy is characterized by increasing interpenetration and the crystallization of transnational markets and structures, the state itself is having to act more and more like a market player, that shapes its policies to promote, control, and maximize returns from market forces in an international setting."

Clear criteria (immigration policy) of who are/are not legitimate citizens of the state are maintained primarily as a strong regulative control over who is permitted access to this community of goods and services. Policy concerning such access is defined almost completely in terms of the performativity requirements of a competition state. For those who are legitimate members of the state, their shared identity is not that of the social citizens of the welfare state, but that of actual or potential contributors to the performativity of the competition state. The trend is thus to turn all nationals into contributors (an active labor market policy), and to define out of existence non-contributors. As Lyotard (1984, xxiv) correctly discerns, the application of the criterion of optimizing the system's performance "to all of our games necessarily entails a certain level of terror, whether soft or hard: be operational (that is commensurable) or disappear."

A state which is oriented in terms of the culture of performativity is a secretive state, oriented to making discreet deals with corporate players who can significantly affect the performativity of this state-centric system. Information is openly shared by the state with its internal environment only to the extent that it furthers strategies of political and social management of the actors within this environment. The consequence of this is that a great deal of the business of the state is private rather than public. Or, to put it more accurately, this business becomes public only as social movements and their minority party representatives within the legislature contest state decisions, and, by so doing, drag them into the visibility of openly contested political representations.

In this context democratic politics is centered in the evanescent openings of public spaces which the new social movements achieve in their contestation of the state's definition of the situation. By turning the techno(econo)cratic representations of state policy into openly contested political issues, they convert performative decisions into rhetorical praxis. Democratic struggle is centered on attempting and effecting this conversion. A politics of representation depends on making issues visible by opening up public spaces. This is why the state has encouraged a high degree of concentration and centralization of print and electronic media capital. However, even within the controlling ambience of a partnership between the state and media corporate players, representational control is never complete. As Michael Ryan (1989, chapter six) argues, vertical use of rhetoric to control meaning by condensing it within a governing metaphor—for example, the USA as the liberator of a Kuwait from a Hitler-like Saddam Hussein—can never foreclose horizontal use of rhetoric where metonymy can develop meanings which work against the vertical integration and condensation of meaning. For example, if the USA state, led by ex-CIA Director Bush, emphasized the liberator ideal of US Manifest Destiny, then it is all too easy for it to become hoist on its own petard in relation to those audiences to whom its rhetoric is addressed. This is what happened with US intervention in Vietnam, when the corruption and antidemocratic features of the Diem regime in South Vietnam belied all the rhetoric on behalf of defending the forces of democracy against those of totalitarianism. Equally, while the Bush-led USA state was intent on ensuring that it was the controlling leader of any liberating intervention in the Gulf (Middle East), it was unable to control the metonymic properties of liberation rhetoric, and thus to explain why it was that it abandoned the Kurds, who rose up against Hussein only to draw down upon themselves his counterforce and military terror.[2]

It will be clear from what I have argued that the performative state has an historical symbiosis with the centricity of both the classical bourgeois liberal/republican state and of the welfare state. The system that is the reference point for the performative criteria of efficiency, economy and effectiveness borrows its cultural and structural integrity from these earlier phases of the modern state's existence. The performative, competition state represents itself as the natural development of the *bürgerliche* culture of public man and of the social citizenship of the welfare state. This representation is an exercise in performativity. It is not substantively anchored in the current commitments and *modus operandi* of the state. State-sponsored police terror, as well as addictive behaviors (alcohol and other drugs, gambling), are used to control and marginalize those who are destined to be non-contributors. The prisons fill up, legal due process becomes a matter of privilege rather than of right, and the Redferns or Harlems of this world are subject to police terror raids that are never called properly to public account.

The performative state empties the formally instituted public sphere of substantive politicized content. Executive decision-making is undertaken in relation to a series of disciplinary instruments, with regard to internal party discussion and parliamentary process: these ensure that public debate and information sharing are never developed beyond a strictly limited theatrical intimation of debate and information sharing. The performative state is the response of vertically integrated control agendas to the conditions of postmodernity. If there cannot be a substantive community of ends shared by a legitimate elite of master subject citizens (the private proprietors of households), and the dissonance of irresolvably multiple perspectives of difference is introduced, the most sensible move is to abandon the substantive game of modern citizenship in favor of performativity.

At the same time, the terms of struggle for democratic politics have changed in ways that are congruent with dissonance, dissension, multiplicity, and difference. They are not oriented to the development and stability of a single political arena or public sphere, if only for the reason that their motivating agendas combine to indicate a complexity and multiplicity that is not containable within the one public space. For all these reasons, democratic discourse that is oriented in terms of a centric public sphere is truly anachronistic.

III

Thus the society of the future falls less within the province of a Newtonian anthropology...than a pragmatics of language particles. There are many different language games—and heterogeneity of elements. They only give rise to institutions in patches—local determinism.
—Jean-François Lyotard, *The Postmodern Condition* 1984

Lyotard (1984, 17) argues that, under postmodern conditions, the social becomes "flexible networks of language games." Politics thus becomes the more or less extensive politicization of these networks, and the situation of the language games involved within public space. A democratic politics is oriented in principle to the development of this politicization within both specific language games, for instance, the language game of service-delivery or the language game of academic pedagogy, and across such flexible networks of language games. It is important to enquire how this democratic politics is situated in respect of a performative culture of governance. Performativity is one type of rhetorical practice; open dialogue, discussion, dissension and sharing of information is another. Where the former reifies certain values, such as efficiency, the latter develops rhetorical praxis by asking basic questions like: efficient in relation to what ends, whose ends, and what time scale (short, medium, long term)?

As we have seen, performativity involves the use of terror, but there are important limits on how far the business of governance can be brought within the ambit of the principle of performativity and its distinctive form of terror. As both Lyotard (1984, 15) and Melucci (1988, 249; 1989, 207) argue, the steering capacity of the system is improved by allowing performativity to be substituted for by the politicization of particular issue areas. With the kind of complexity that the contemporary state has to deal with, and where policy decisions serve to effectively reduce this complexity by making provisional commitments, this reduction needs to be well informed if it is to work. Social movements are both reliable and creative in making visible the issues that have to be faced. For example, it is no good thinking that aged care service delivery can work in one mode if it turns out to be culturally unacceptable to those who need the service. Melucci's characterization of the "new" social movements, which are engaged as contestants of the performative state, emphasizes their primary feature as movements engaged in symbolic challenge. These movements open and develop a politics of representation, and thereby contribute to converting performative decisions into rhetorical praxis. Melucci (1988, 247) states:

> The modern contemporary phenomena to which I refer (in particular the women's movement, the environmental 'movements', the forms of youth collective action and the mobilizations in favor of peace) are not concerned primarily with citizenship. This is not to say that this theme has disappeared. In the collective action of women, for example, the problem of rights, inequality and exclusion constitute a large part of the mobilization process. But what women, along with other contemporary political actors, have achieved is above all to practice alternative definitions of sense: in other words, they have created meanings and definitions of identity which contrast with the increasing determination of individual and collective life by impersonal technocratic power.

These movements are themselves flexible networks of language games rather than a precisely bounded, hierarchically integrated organizational presence. They are subject to an internal politics of multiple and conflicting representations of why they exist, what it is that they should do, and how they should operate. Perhaps more significantly, a good deal of movement activity is submerged within the commonsense of everyday life. This permits dissenting constructions of the movement's politics to assume peaceful coexistence in the form of different and plural ways of conducting everyday life.

Mobilization is in terms of a flexible, networked membership, and it is understood that the sites of struggle are themselves multiple. Accordingly, for these movements, there is not public space neatly sequestered and bounded in relation to private space. Kitchen table conversation can become a public space, not because those using it are planning their next political action, but because their discussion and debate are politicizing their interaction and relationships. With feminism, for example, public spaces open up in respect of how housework is distributed, and how sexuality is expressed.

These are movements grounded in everyday life: recall the disability movements and their inevitable immersion in fundamental issues of embodiment and survival. They enjoy a resilience because of this. If, for the time being, a movement loses visibility on a larger canvas—for example, the performance art of street demonstrations, which gains prime time electronic media coverage—and if the state substitutes performative criteria for the movement's presence within substantive policy, it is still developing and experimenting within what Melucci terms the latency of everyday life. It is this that makes these movements such a rich source of system innovation and development. As Melucci (1989, 208) puts it:

> The submerged networks of social movements are laboratories of experience. New problems and questions are posed. New answers are invented and tested, and reality is perceived and named in different ways.

> All these experiences are displayed publicly only within particular conjunctures and only by means of the organizing activities described by resource organization theory. But none of this public activity would be possible without the laboratory experiences of the submerged networks.[3]

Social movements and their capacity to open up public spaces of openly contested representations are, then, necessary for the principle of performativity to operate. They enhance what Melucci (1989, 207) terms the "already high learning capacity or "reflexitivity" of complex systems. This is why, instead of responding to the backward looking nostalgia of conservative groups for racial homogeneity, the state maintains an equal opportunity relationship to difference, thereby maintaining open access to critical information about the changing demographics, markets and environments of the system. It is also why the public management of relatively new service areas such as home and community care maintains a consultative relationship to the field of consumers and carers.

Performativity thus depends on the perviousness of the policy-making capacities of the state to social movements which represent emergent demands and issues for the system. For this reason, a performative state cannot insulate itself against politics. If performative terror lies in the rationality of "be operational (that is, commensurable) or disappear," the requirement to be operational simultaneously militates against the adoption of widely visible, class-nondiscriminatory and systemic terror. For these reasons the performative state is more of a democratic than a police state. It maintains rhetorical continuity with the traditions of liberal/republican democracy and with social democracy as a way of both signalling and explaining its perviousness to social movements.

Melucci (1988) sees social movements as engaging in primarily symbolic contestation which challenges dominant representations, the effect of which is to make power visible and accountable within the public space opened up by this contestation. The decision-makers absorb this contestation within policies which take up as well as neutralize the challenge. These policies are the negotiated settlements to which I have referred above: "They have to be redefined continually and rapidly because the differences change, the conflicts shift, the agreements cease to satisfy and new forms of domination are constantly emerging" (Melucci, 1988, 251).

Their force is local in both a temporal and relational sense, temporally local, for the reasons Melucci has just indicated, and relationally local, because the fields of force out of which negotiated settlements come are themselves local in relation to the system. Performativity is the only principle available which permits some degree of commensurability across different contexts of pressure for complexity-reducing decisions. It thereby assumes a pan-local force, which does not shield it from being upset in a particular, local context of struggle.

Melucci and Lyotard emphasize the relational properties of symbolic contestation and language games. This is a semiotic politics which shows how it is possible that social movements can convert dominant codes and powerful organizations to their own purposes, purposes, it is clear, that are no more exclusively within the control of those movements than dominant agendas are within the control of those movements, rhetorical antagonists. In this sense, symbolic co-optation can work in both directions. This is why Melucci (1989, 208, emphasis in the original) distinguishes his view of power from that of Foucault, Deleuze and Guattari: "They share a one-dimensional view of power—as the construction and administration of subjects—whereas reality as we experience it in complex societies is in my opinion the resultant of powerful organizations which attempt to define the meaning of reality *and* actors and networks of actors who use the resources of these same organizations to define reality in novel ways."

Local determinism is a principle of institutionalization which elides the two alternatives Adam Smith offered in *The Wealth of Nations:* the invisible hand of the market, or the "men of system" who attempt to arrange society as though it were pieces on a chess board in accordance with a grand plan or vision. For Smith, the former option had the singular virtue of working through the intentionality of individuals participating in a self-interested relationship to exchange transactions with others. Local determinism indicates a different principle of sociality: a language game: "the question of the social bond, insofar as it is a question, is itself a language game, the game of inquiry. It immediately positions the person who asks, as well as the addressee and the referent asked about: it is already the social bond" (Lyotard, 1984, 15).

A language game is institutionalized when it functions according to constraints which regulate what is admissible within the game and how moves in the game are to be made (Lyotard, 1984, 17). As with the policies Melucci discusses, this institutionalization has a provisional and conjunctural character: "the limits the institution imposes on potential language 'moves' are never established once and for all (even if they have been formally defined)" (Lyotard, 1984, 17).[4] As Lyotard argues, the limits themselves are the stakes in the game. The language game of home and community care service delivery is one in which the limits are under constant tussle. Not least do these concern, as we have seen, who is authorized to speak, and on behalf of whom. In aged care, most medical professionals would like to reinstate a game in which the needy individuals are positioned as "patients," as those of whom questions may be asked by the professional but who are accorded no right to ask questions themselves of the professional or any other participant in the service delivery language game.

IV

We must arrive at an idea and practice of justice that is not linked to that of consensus.
—Jean-François Lyotard, *The Postmodern Condition* 1984

What, indeed, is the status of justice under the conditions of postmodern politics? I have argued that postmodern politics is constituted by a field of tension and conflict between, on the one hand, an open politics of voice and representation, and, on the other, performativity as a principle of selective closure in respect of the information overload and social complexity which confronts the contemporary state. I have suggested also that the new social movements of the kind which are theorized by Melucci are movements oriented within an imaginary of resistance to domination combined with a commitment to self-determination. Moreover, these movements situate themselves within a polyphony of different movement claims to self-determination and resistance to the performative terror of the state. That is, they share a practical understanding of the universality of the political ethic which informs these claims: they understand both their affinity with each other as similar though distinct claimants of this kind, and they are aware that the state is either relatively open to the ethos they share, or closed.

At the same time, these movements do not resile from their differences, which make their claims of self-determination and resistance to domination non-additive and non-totalizable. They are not subsumable within a single culture, ethos, or vision of emancipation or self-determination. There is no way they could agree on a shared conception of justice, although it is possible for them to explore the connections and even the overlaps between their respective conceptions of justice.

For example, a feminist politics rhetorically embraces all women regardless of their positioning in relation to racist relations of domination. It is, thus, impossible for a feminist politics to be mapped onto an anti-racist politics, which necessarily rhetorically embraces all Black Australians (Americans),Maori, or whichever constituency is involved. However, this does not preempt a Black American feminist such as Barbara Smith from exploring the connections, as well as the differences, in her feminist, anti-racist politics when it is addressed to white, Jewish feminists and when it is addressed to Black women in the context of a complicated historical relationship between these two oppressed groups within the United States.[5] In focusing on relationships between Black and Jewish women, Smith (1984, 69) declares:

> Because of the inherent complexities of this subject, one of the things I found
> most overwhelming was the sense that I had to be writing for two distinct
> audiences at the same time. I was very aware that what I want to say [about
> black anti-Semitism] to other Black women is properly part of an 'in-house'
> discussion and it undoubtedly would be a lot more comfortable for us if
> somehow the act of writing did not require it to go public. With Jewish
> women, on the other hand, although we may have a shared bond of feminism,
> what I say comes from a position outside the group. It is impossible for me to
> forget that in speaking to Jewish women I am speaking to white women, a
> role complicated by a racist tradition of Black people repeatedly having to
> teach white people about the meaning of oppression. I decided then to write
> sections that would cover what I need to say to Black women and what I need
> to say to Jewish women, fully understanding that this essay would be read in
> its entirety by both Black and Jewish women, as well as by individuals from a
> variety of other backgrounds.

Difference in, and sometimes connections between, emancipatory agendas indicate a kind of universalism. This is not, however, the universalism of a modern, rationalist emancipatory politics. The legitimacy of these multiple and different emancipatory claims does not reside in reason. There is no shared community of reason because there is no collective, universal subject.

In this context, should reason be claimed by adherents to modernist emancipatory traditions as the arbiter of political claims, it must be perceived as an arbitrary closure of debate, an exclusion of difference, a nostalgic assertion of a homogeneous subject that has lost all credibility. The construction of a collective homogeneous subject becomes perforce a politics of the right, which moves to defend not the universality of the human subject but the particularity of the Western (white, European) subject against those who are represented, in Margaret Thatcher's phrase, as belonging to "alien cultures." The right appropriates the language of difference and resituates it within an unapologetic celebration of Western racism. Thus, while the integration of Europe is bringing the dismantling of intra-European national restrictions on the movement of Europeans within Europe, immigration restrictions on the entry of non-Europeans (blacks, Third World peoples) have intensified.[6] If the Kurds, or any other people within what Western racism terms "the Third World," should become persecuted and subject to genocidal terror, they are not to be accorded refuge as immigrants within the nations of the West.

Western racism thus appropriates from modern social science the imaginary of a differential common culture and defends its integrity against alien incursions. This is a consensualism of a familiar kind: by excluding the alien other, differences at home are also suppressed, and the order of the modern West is upheld.

This point underlines a critical feature of the new social movements and their espousal of a non-consensualist politics of difference. These movements do not conduct themselves in terms of an homogeneous movement identity in relation to which individual adherents discipline and subject themselves. They eschew the idea of a shared or common culture. Instead, the identity of a movement arises out of a politics of affinity (Haraway, 1990) between subjects who continually reinterpret the movement and its goals in relation to the changing character of their own personal histories:

> In other words, these different forms of consciousness are grounded...in one's personal history; but that history—one's identity—is interpreted or reconstructed by each of us within the horizon of meanings and knowledges available in the culture at given historical moments, a horizon that also includes modes of political commitment and struggle. Self and identity, in other words, are always grasped and understood within particular discursive configurations. Consciousness, therefore, is never fixed, never attained once and for all, because discursive boundaries change with historical conditions (de Lauretis 1986: 8; and see Martin and Mohanty 1986).

A self which is discursively oriented to "the understanding of identity as multiple and even self-contradictory" (de Lauretis, 1986, 9) is clearly incapable of practicing the disciplinary self-government of a self oriented within a culture of self-mastery (mastery by reason of the passions, instincts or drives). The former self is one which understands and resists the exclusionary terror of self-mastery whereby the integrity of a self is established through the exclusion and repression of all that is rigidly deemed non-self. Martin and Mohanty (1986, 1987) show how Minnie Bruce Pratt's autobiographical narrative enables reflection on postmodern selfhood:

> Pratt's own histories are in constant flux. There is no linear progression—based on 'that old view', no developmental notion of her own identity or self. There is instead a constant expansion of her 'constricted eye', a necessary reevaluation and return to the past in order to move forward to the present. Geography, demography, and architecture, as well as the configuration of her relationships to particular people (her father, her lover, her workmate), serve to indicate the fundamentally relational nature of identity and the negations on which the assumption of a singular, fixed and essential self is based. For the narrator, such negativity is represented by a rigid identity such as that of her father, which sustains its appearance of stability by defining itself in terms of what it is not: not black, not female, not Jewish, not Catholic, not poor, etc. The 'self' in this narrative is not an essence or truth concealed by patriarchal layers of deceit and lying in wait of discovery, revelation or birth.

A non-consensualist politics of difference develops rhetorical procedures which problematize a subject speaking on behalf of another, and which put a premium on subjects finding their own "voice" within whatever politics of representation is at hand. Within this politics, subjects are understood to be discursively positioned within the conjunctural historical moment of contested narratives of who they are and where they are going. Thus, with feminism operating as a discursive intervention within this contestation, females are accorded a shared positioning as women. It follows that, in any cross-gender politics, women must be accorded a voice in that politics. From the point of view of this politics, how women distribute the representation of this voice amongst themselves is up to them. Necessarily, however, this representation is subject to an internal feminist politics of difference, and of making those who speak as women accountable to their complex and differentiated constituency. This is achieved by ensuring that as many differently positioned women speak "on behalf of women" as there are discursively posited differences among women. They may arrive at a negotiated settlement of their differences in what is represented, not as unicity, but as a claim on cross-gender political process which they share for the time being.

It is important to understand that a negotiated settlement may, more often than not, represent a willingness to achieve pragmatic compromise in relation to coexistent and different views of justice. For example, this is the case in New Zealand where Maori and Pakeha do not share the same conception of justice. Andrew Sharp (1990, 1–2) eloquently represents the nature of this pragmatic compromise in respect of "those who decided to argue less about the strict demands of justice and more about how to live together in conditions of severe disagreement about what those demands were":

> They were less concerned...with rights and duties (and with who should have authority) than as to what it might be a good idea to do; and they were considerably less heroic in their clarity of definition and imperativeness of demand. They spoke of deals and settlements that could be lived with rather than speaking the language of justice. They spoke more of politics than the state. Unwilling to say that one or other conception of justice must predominate, they sought political settlements, impermanent no doubt, but which would enable the peoples to continue to live together in tolerable harmony. They argued that New Zealand was not exclusively a Pakeha land, nor Aotearoa exclusively Maori. They were happy to fudge questions of rights and of sovereignty.
>
> In fact, and despite their obvious contradictoriness, the two logics were often fused in practice. The same people adopted both and argued each with equal conviction; the demands of justice and the desirability of imperfect settlement were asserted together in single documents or single tracts of speech. And in all this there were no great signs of strain. If this was perversity, it was a perversity deeply natural to the New Zealander.

Within the spirit of this kind of politics, "tradition" or "identity" are invoked in order to ground claims, but, as we have seen, there is a non-essentialist understanding of tradition and identity. These are subject to the conjunctural rhetorical play of the claims themselves, and this is understood, up to a point, by the players. Thus, for example, the Treaty of Waitangi in its Maori language version is invoked by Maori as a founding document for their claims on justice, but they do not invoke the document in terms of the conventions of (Maori) meaning operative at the time it was signed. Instead, their invocation of it rewrites the Treaty in terms of contemporary meaning where, for example, Maori invocation of traditional rights comes to include rights framed in terms of the social citizenship of the welfare state and the more recent discourse of social equity (see Sharp, 1990, 134–140). Sharp (1990, 135–136, emphasis in the original), comments on the "anachronistic extensions of intended meaning" of the Treaty: "certainly an impulse behind the extension of the concept of 'taonga' [all that is treasured by Maori] to include the language, culture and education *in 1840* was not so much one to rewrite (wrongly) the history of the signing of the Treaty for its own sake, but rather that of bringing injustices to the Maori under the aegis of breach of contract."

In this context, the rhetoric of being Maori assumes a polysemic existence which varies from one context to another. In one context, Maori may signify black in contradistinction to white (Pakeha). This, however, does not stop lesbian separatist Pakeha feminists being redefined as black (Maori) by Maori lesbian separatist feminists in accordance with a rhetorical map that makes metonymic association between patriarchy, whiteness, and colonialism (see Dominy, 1990). Similarly, in contexts of environmental politics, Maori may signify Green, thereby permitting Pakeha environmentalists identification with what it means to be Maori.

V

A recognition of the heteromorphous nature of language games is a first step in that direction. This obviously implies a renunciation of terror, which assumes that they are isomorphic and tries to make them so. The second step is the principle that any consensus on the rules defining a game and the 'moves' playable within it must be local, in other words, agreed on by its present players and subject to eventual cancellation. The orientation then favors a multiplicity of finite meta-arguments, by which I mean argumentation that concerns metaprescriptives and is limited in space and time.
—Jean-François Lyotard, *The Postmodern Condition* 1984

I have undertaken here a series of meditations on and applications of Lyotard's *The Postmodern Condition* with the intention of outlining some of the most important aspects of a postmodern politics. This is a politics which comprises a number of interlocking fields of force. One such field opposes the principle of performativity to that of rhetorical praxis. This field is bound up with the politics of the state, where the state is the site of struggle. Another field opposes a consensualist politics of difference on behalf of the West to a non-consensualist politics which is oriented within a postcolonial ethos. A further field opposes modernist rhetorics of democratic, rationalist consensus to postmodern rhetorics of local, conjunctural, multiple agreements, context-bound, and varying by context.

These fields of force evoke, as they reinterpret and resituate, modern visions and traditions of politics. At the same time, they are still barely theorized. Dominant constructions of the polity and politics are still those of Western modernity. There is good reason for this: it is a functional state of affairs for those who experience a non-consensualist politics of difference as cultural loss. However, many so situated are still committed to democratic values in ways which permit new learning. It is important that those of us situated so as to find, rather than to lose, voice in the new politics proceed to reflect on and theorize it. Only then can we offer a bridge from a modern to a postmodern democratic politics. Only then also can our reflection on emergent practice permit us to develop and refine our strategic interventions.

Notes

1 The Epistemological Politics of Postmodern Feminist Theorizing

1   John (1989, 63) proceeds to make some very suggestive and insightful propositions: "Indeed, feminism could be described as a narrative about the discovery *of*
representation itself—from the prior moment when women's identity as women
was either largely accepted or disregarded to a time of making it their subject, politically and interpretatively."

2   For this interpretation of feminism, see Haraway (1990), Nicholson (1990),
Nicholson and Fraser (1990), de Lauretis (1988) and Haraway (1988). For a broad-
er construction of the new social movements of the metropolis, as a response to the
presence of a colonized other within the United States (Afro-Americans) see
Wallace (1989).

3   De Lauretis's (1988, 135–136) analysis is apposite: "While the axis of gender, historically the first epistemological ground of feminism, defines a form of
consciousness based on the opposition of woman to man, and the oppression of
women by men, and hence produces a relatively stable or unified feminist subject
defined by its consciousness of gender oppression as a one-way power relation
(where women are the victims and thus the revolutionary class subject, so to
speak), the other axes, by their very interrelatedness and co-implication in gender
and in one another, define another form of consciousness, what I will call a consciousness of complicity, in particular, of ideological complicity."

4   See the book on the exhibition *Hans Haacke: Unfinished Business,* edited by Brian
Wallis (1986), which includes an essay by Frederic Jameson on "Hans Haacke and
the Cultural Logic of Postmodernism."

5   This is suggested by the following exchange (Foster, 1987, 114) around Silvia
Kolbowski's challenge to Crimp (initials have been converted to full names):

> Dan Graham: ...one of the forms that an imported deconstruction takes
> on is puritanical—I mean a self-referential questioning of motives and
> positions, and endless, tautological examination of self-consciousness and

123

conscience. This idea of the correct 'position', politically speaking, of the 'correct' I.

Silvia Kolbowski: I think you're speaking in different terms than I am. What I have in mind is not puritanical in the least.

Dan Graham: I'm not negative about puritanism. Self-questioning is what we're doing now—not only Silvia, everybody....But there's a certain circularity here.

Barbara Kruger: To me puritanism is about a desire to pull everything back to one thing: to say, 'To say this is not historically grounded, not politically correct, not properly footnoted...but that is exemplary.' Puritanism reduces things to a univocal voiceover or dictation of fact. Why not allow for a number of different voices, a number of different positions—a horizontal rather than a vertical, hierarchical structure?

Silvia Kolbowski: Voices and position that might question each other as well.

Barbara Kruger: Exactly.

2 Postmodern Epistemological Politics and Social Science

1   Charles Lemert's (1988, 803–804) sympathetic portrayal of contemporary challenges to "the most fundamental categories of social thought" reproduces this exclusion:

> ...the epistemological uppitiness of feminist theory may well be one of its more important contributions to feminist theory. The fact of exclusion from the disciplines is, presumably, the political as well as the organizational condition for the clarity and probity of much feminist theory. Many feminists in institutionally marginal programs, often in other than first-rank universities, subjected to well-known secret doubts about the 'objectivity' of their knowledge have been forced to develop a theory and practice of knowledge consistent with the social experience of exclusion. Hence the critical difference of feminist theory."

Lemert here is uncritically reproducing the binary opposition of inner and outer; nowhere is this more evident than in the familiar trick on the part of the powerful (the "included") in conferring on the excluded the status of being more moral (more innocent, more idealistic, etc.).

2   Spivak's (1989, 217–218, emphases in the original) comments are apt here: "It is *in the interest of* diagnosing the ontological ruse, on the basis of which there is oppression of woman, that we have to bring our understanding of the relationship between the name 'woman' and deconstruction into crisis. If we do not take the time to understand this in our zeal to be 'political', then I fear we act out the kind of play that Nietzsche figured out in *The Genealogy of Morals:* in the interest of giving an alibi to his desire to punish, which is written into his way of being, in other words in the interest of a survival game, man produces an alibi which is

called justice. And in the interests of that alibi, man has to define and articulate, over and over again, the name of man."

3   One of the nastiest moves to discredit Said, for example, has been to point out that he shares in the authority of the metropolitan, intellectual elite by his institutional position within one of the metropolitan, elite universities (for discussion of this see Marcus, 1990, 7). As Marcus points out, where Said is positioned as a Palestinian, a less than innocent signifier in the current setting, those who attack him in this way never position themselves (see, e.g., Turner, 1989).

3 The Place of Women's Studies in the Contemporary University

1   I owe the first point to Nancy Cott's (1987) chapter on "Professionalism and Feminism" in *The Grounding of Modern Feminism*. Cott (p. 216) remarks: "Because of the close relations of the professions to education and service (where women's contributions were acknowledged to an extent); and because the professions promised neutral standards of judgment for both sexes, collegial autonomy, and horizons for growth, they became a magnet among the potential areas of paid employment for women."

2   Cott (1987, 234–235) suggests that "the impact of the Civil Rights Act of 1964 in effectuating feminist protests within and about the professions in the 1960s and 1970s cannot be minimized; women in the earlier generations had no such support from outside the professions themselves."

3   There are a number of important contributions to this important self-critical insight, notably: Judith Butler (1990), *Gender Trouble*; Denise Riley (1988), *"Am I That Name?" Feminism and the Category of "Women" in History*; Elizabeth Grosz (1990), "Contemporary Theories of Power and Subjectivity." Grosz (1990,59, emphases in the original) proposes: "To say something is *not* true, valuable, or useful *without posing alternatives* is, paradoxically, to affirm that it *is* true....Thus coupled with this negative project or rather, indistinguishable from it, must be a positive, constructive project: creating alternatives, producing *feminist*, not simply *anti-sexist*, theory."

4   Young's (1990a) critique of the "metaphysics of presence" in the ideal of community is "The Ideal of Community and the Politics of Difference" in *Feminism/Postmodernism*. Her development of a democratic politics of difference is to be found in her (1990b) *Justice and the Politics of Difference*. It is noteworthy that her development of democratic theory *as* a politics of difference is predicated on her acceptance of the limits of her own positioning as one which requires her to dialogue and connect with differently positioned movement actors: "As a white, heterosexual, middle-class, able-bodied, not old woman, I cannot claim to speak for radical movements of Blacks, Latinos, American Indians, poor people, lesbians, old people, or the disabled. But the political commitment to social justice which motivates my philosophical reflection tells me that I also cannot speak without them. Thus while my personal passion begins with feminism, and I reflect on the experience and ideas of the peace, environmental, and anti-intervention movements in

which I have participated, the positions I develop...emerge from reflection on the experience and ideas of movements of other oppressed groups, insofar as I can understand that experience by reading and talking with people in them. Thus while I do not claim here to speak for all reasonable persons [a reference to the universal standpoint of liberal and republican democratic theory], I do aim to speak from multiple positions and on the basis of the experience of several contemporary social movements (*ibid.*, p.14)." This insight might be developed to become one of investigating and understanding what I call the reciprocal interpellations of the social movements of the contemporary present: e.g. it is arguable that the postcolonial, national liberation and anti-racist movements not only called each other into being but they did so in respect of feminism as well, albeit indirectly.

5 Pratt's piece appears in Elly Bulkin, Minnie Bruce Pratt and Barbara Smith (1984) *Yours in Struggle: Three Feminist Perspectives on Anti-Semitism and Racism.* Biddy Martin and Chandra Mohanty offer an insightful commentary on it in the collection edited by Teresa de Lauretis (1986), *Feminist Studies/Critical Studies*, where de Lauretis herself picks up on both in her Introduction. Together these pieces constitute a mini-tradition of feminist theory.

6 Equally, the university cannot require that she deny the ways in which her values and politics inform her teaching and scholarship. All it can require is that these ways are accountable to critically reflective, analytical and evidential procedures.

4 Beyond Natural Right: The Conditions for Universal Citizenship

For helpful comments on the original version I am particularly grateful to David Levine, Joan Landes, and an anonymous referee for Social Concept.

1 Here I draw on statements by Locke in *Two Treatises of Government* (1965, 334, par. 35, and 200, par. 33). For an extended argument concerning the emergence of the discourse of action in the work of Locke, Hobbes, Rousseau, and Montesquieu, see Yeatman (1980).

2 Consider in this context these propositions of Hobbes (1968, 217):

> A person is to be whose words or actions are considered, either as his own, or as representing the words or actions of another man, or of any other thing to whom they are attributed, whether truly or by Fiction.

> When they are considered as his own, then he is called a Natural Person: And when they are considered as representing the words and actions of an other, then is he a Feigned or Artificial person.

3 Extended argument to this effect is made by Talcott Parsons in *The Structure of Social Action* (1968), especially in ch. 3.

4 Though I have said above...that all Men by Nature are equal, I cannot be supposed to understand all sorts of Equality: Age or Virtue may give Men a just Precedency: Excellence of Parts and Merit may place others above the

Common Level: Birth may subject some, and Alliance or Benefits others, to pay an Observance to those to whom Nature, Gratitude or other Respects may have made it due; *and yet all this consists with the Equality, which all Men are in, in respect of Jurisdiction or Dominion* one over another...being that equal Right that every Man hath, to his Natural Freedom, without being subjected to the Will or Authority of any other Men. Locke (1965, 346, par. 54, emphasis added).

5   Evidence for this interpretation of Durkheim's position can be found in his "Preface to the Second Edition" of *The Division of Labor in Society* (1964, 1–32). While Durkheim accepts that employers and employees have different interests and, therefore, should have their own respective associations, he argues that within any one industry there must be an industry association bringing together employer and employee groups.

6   While I will not argue this here, I would propose that Rawls's *Theory of Justice* (1971) is a creative combination of the Social Contract idea and this modified theory of natural right. In both respects, his theory of justice does not go beyond natural right.

7   This classification of Durkheim's broad conception of a moral education into its cognitive, moral, and affective components is Talcott Parsons's (1964).

8   Marshall delivered these as the Marshall Lectures, Cambridge, 1949.

6 State and Community

1   *Pakeha* is the other term of the Maori/white settler colonist binary relationship. Maori regard themselves as the *tangata whenua* of New Zealand/Aotearoa, namely the original inhabitants or people of the land. While Pakeha signifies whiteness, as the following quotation bears out, it also signifies what is construed as an integrity of belonging to New Zealand/Aotearoa through putting roots down in a way that brings about commitment to this national society. Thus, while I as a white-Australian living in New Zealand qualified in one respect for membership of this category, my maintenance of an Australian identity and intent to return to Australia before long disqualified me for membership. The following entry for "Pakeha (Foreigner, White New Zealander)" is from a Maori-authored bilingual text *Tikanga Whakaaro: Key Concepts in Māori Culture* (Barlow, 1991, 87):

> Pākehā is the name that was given by the Māori to the white-skinned immigrants who came from the United Kingdom and settled New Zealand. The name also refers to Patupaiarehe or fairy.

> Perhaps the reason why the first white people were called Pākehā by the Māori was that the strangers who arrived on their ships appeared to look like fairies or fair-skinned supernatural beings. The word Pākehā can also signify a flea or type of eel. But in my view the term as applied to white people did not derive from any of these alternative meanings. The word is not a term of denigration in Maori usage, but rather one of respect in asso-

ciating the new settlers with supernatural beings or god-like people (at least in terms of their appearance).

These days the word Pākehā is not used for all foreigners, only those who have white skin. Further distinctions are made between white races such as Germans, Russians, Australians, and so forth. Other foreigners such as Japanese, Asians, Polynesians, or Africans are never referred to as Pākehā They are usually called by the name of the country to which they belong; for example, a person from Japan would be called a Japanese. Again the genuine Pākehā are those original immigrants who came from the United Kingdom and settled this country.

Many white settler New Zealanders reject the term Pakeha for themselves and insist on the generality of the category "New Zealander." For discussion of self-identified Pakeha as an ethnic response to Maori sovereignty claims, see Spoonley, 1992. The three terms most often used in official and media sub-classifications of New Zealanders are Maori, Pakeha or European, and Pacific Islander. Either way ethnic differences among white settlers or European New Zealanders are occluded, and those who do not fit any of these categories are left as a residual category. Ethnic differences *within* Maori (and Pacific Islanders) are also occluded. Here it will become evident that my defense of conventionalism is at some considerable odds with the customary and kinship-oriented rhetoric of Aboriginals or Indigenous peoples as the first or original nations within the postcolonial state formations of Australia and New Zealand. On the other hand, I believe it to be possible to undertake a conventionalist approach to the claims of these "nations within" (for this terminology, see Fleras and Elliott, 1992).

7 Postmodernity and Revisioning the Political

1   I know this area fairly well: I was the consultant who did the joint Commonwealth and State Government sponsored evaluation (1989) of the largest Home and Community Care service type in South Australia: Domiciliary Care. Home and Community Care (HACC) refers to the joint government funded program which is designed to keep people with moderate to severe disabilities, who are in need of assistance with the tasks of everyday living, at home for as long as possible. This is motivated by both cost-management reasons in the demographic context of a rapidly aging population and by a value commitment to individual autonomy.

2   In a newspaper report *(The Australian,* April 8, 1991) a *Sunday Times* syndicated article states that: "The decision not to intervene was based on two factors: a reluctance to get embroiled in a lengthy Iraqi civil war, and warnings against intervention from Saudi Arabia, Turkey and Egypt, which feared that a splintered Iraq could lead to permanent instability in the region." It also states that: "Many US soldiers [in the at-that-time US occupied zone in Southern Iraq] are unhappy about their role." At a checkpoint near Basra, Sergeant Paul Conrad, 27, said: "The people of Kuwait asked us for help against Saddam and we gave it. Now the people of Iraq are asking us for help and we should give it to them too. What is the difference?"

3   "Resource mobilization theory emphasizes the fundamental importance of factors such as the availability of resources—recruitment networks, the costs and benefits of participation, organizations, funding and the availability of professionals—in analyzing the recent growth of social movements" (Interviewers, in Melucci, 1989, 192).

4   "Reciprocally, it can be said that the boundaries only stabilize when they cease to be stakes in the game" (Lyotard, 1984, 17).

5   Smith (1984, 71–72) offers an explanation of this relationship which is true not only of the United States to which she refers but also of South Africa: "I think that both Black and Jewish people expect more from each other than they do from white people generally or from gentiles generally...Our respective 'awareness of oppression' leads us to believe that each other's communities should 'know better' than to be racist or anti-semitic because we have first-hand knowledge of bigotry and discrimination. This partially explains the disproportionate anger and blame we may feel when the other group displays attitudes much like those of the larger society." Both the US and South African Communist Parties have attracted a disproportionate number of Jews, and have been identified with cross-race political organizing.

6   Evelyn Pisier (1990, 105) discusses the development of a racist politics of difference in the French context: "'National preference' is becoming a 'response to immigration'. Beyond all avowed racism, 'the right to difference' suffices to justify theoretically that one 'keep their hands off my [French] people.' The 'new' racism is henceforth 'differentialist' and 'the right to difference', as commonly employed by third-worldists in the 1960's is literally recuperated and turned around in the name of a 'Western shedding of guilt.' Since even on the left one has recognized that 'the right of peoples' has become the principle [sic] instrument for strangling 'the Rights of Man', and since third-worldism is 'in question', and since it is necessary to 'get over one's bad conscience' as a privileged Westerner and over the perverse effects of the 'West as Welfare State for the World', the right moment came for the right to affirm the principle of national preference: confronting the 'massive arrival of immigrants from the Third World', coupled with the primordial concern 'to defend the identity and sovereignty of the nation', it suddenly became necessary (said the right-wing 'Club de l'Horloge' in 1985) to 'differentiate the situation of foreigners from that of citizens', to rework the code of nationality, 'to expel illegal aliens and those whose visas have expired', and to reserve 'for French the benefit of legislation conceived in relation to their needs and for the development of their country.'"

Consolidated Bibliography

Adorno, T., et al. *The Positivist Dispute in German Sociology*. London: Heinemann Educational Books, 1976.

Anderson, B. *Imagined Communities*, revised edition. London: Verso, 1991.

Anzaldua, G. *Borderlands: La Frontera*. San Francisco: Spinsters/Aunt Lute Company, 1987.

Barlow, C. *Tikanga Whakaaro: Key Concepts in Māori Culture*. Auckland: Oxford University Press, 1991.

Bauman, Z. *Legislators and Interpreters: On Modernity, Post-modernity and Intellectuals*. Ithaca: Cornell University Press, 1987.

Benjamin, A., ed. *Judging Lyotard*. London: Routledge, 1992.

Blustein, J. *Parents and Children: The Ethics of the Family*. Oxford University Press, 1982.

Bottomley, G., M. de Lepervance and J. Martin, eds. *Intersexions: Gender, Race, Ethnicity and Class*. Sydney: Allen & Unwin, 1991.

Bulkin, E., M. Pratt and B. Smith. *Yours in Struggle: Three Feminist Perspectives on Anti-Semitism and Racism*. New York: Long Haul Press, 1984.

Burbules, N., and S. Rice. "Dialogue across Differences: Continuing the Conversation." *Harvard Educational Review* 61,(4): 393–417 (1991).

Butler, J. *Gender Trouble*. New York & London: Routledge, 1990.

Castells, M. *The Informational: City Information Technology, Economic Restructuring and the Urban-Regional Process*. Oxford: Blackwell, 1989.

Cerny, P. *The Changing Architecture of Politics: Structure, Agency and the Future of the State*. London: Sage, 1990.

Chodorow, N. *The Reproduction of Mothering: Psychoanalysis and the Sociology of Gender*. Berkeley: University of California Press, 1978.

Chodorow, N. "Beyond Drive Theory: Object Relations and the Limits of Radical Individualism." *Theory and Society* 14 (3): (1985).

Cott, N. , *The Grounding of Modern Feminism*. New Haven & London: Yale University Press, 1987.

De Lauretis, T. "Feminist Studies/Critical Studies: Issues, Terms, and Contexts." In *Feminist Studies/Critical Studies,* edited by T. de Lauretis. Bloomington: Indiana University Press, 1986.

De Lauretis, T. "Displacing Hegemonic Discourses: Reflections on Feminist Theory in the 1980's." *Inscriptions* 3/4: 127–145 (1988).

De Lauretis, T. "Eccentric Subjects: Feminist Theory and Historical Consciousness." *Feminist Studies* 16 (1): 115–151, (1990).

Derrida, J. "The Ends of Man." In *Margins of Philosophy,* edited by Dr. Alan Bass. Brighton, Sussex: Harvester Press, 1982.

Dick, B. *Search: A Participative Community Planning Process.* Brisbane, Queensland: Interchange, 1989.

Dominy, Michelle. "Maori Sovereignty: A Feminist Invention of Tradition." In *Cultural Identity and Ethnicity in the Pacific,* edited by J. Linnekin and L. Poyer. University of Hawaii Press, 1990.

Donzelot, J. *The Policing of Families.* London: Hutchinson, 1979.

Durkheim, E. *Professional Ethics and Civic Morals.* London: Routledge & Kegan Paul, 1957.

Durkheim, E. *The Division of Labor in Society.* New York: Free Press, 1964.

Elshtain, J. "Sovereignty, Identity, Sacrifice." *Social Research* 58: 545–565 (1991).

Fabian, J. *Time and the Other: How Anthropology Makes Its Object.* New York: Columbia University Press, 1983.

Fabian, J. "Presence and Representation: The Other and Anthropological Writing." *Critical Inquiry* 16: 753–773 (1990).

Finch, J., and D. Groves, eds. *A Labor of Love: Women, Work and Caring.* Routledge and Kegan Paul, London, 1983.

Fleras, A., and J.L. Elliott. *The Nations Within: Aboriginal-State Relations in Canada, the United States and New Zealand.* Toronto: Oxford University Press, 1992.

Foster, H., ed. *Dia Art Foundation Discussions in Contemporary Culture Number One.* Seattle: Bay Press, 1987.

Fraser, N., and L. Nicholson. "Social Criticism Without Philosophy: An Encounter Between Feminism and Postmodernism." In *Feminism/Postmodernism,* edited by L. Nicholson. New York and London: Routledge, 1990.

Gatens, M. "Feminism, Philosophy and Riddles without Answers." In *Feminist Challenges: Social and Political Theory,* edited by C. Pateman and E. Grosz. Sydney: Allen and Unwin, 1986.

Gatens, M. "Towards a Feminist Philosophy of the Body." In *Crossing Boundaries: Feminisms and the Critique of Knowledge,* edited by B. Caine, E. Grosz and M. de Lepervanche. Sydney: Allen and Unwin, 1988.

Gouldner, A. *The Future of Intellectuals and the Rise of the New Class.* Macmillan, London and Basingstoke 1979.

Grosz, E. "The In(ter)vention of Feminist Knowledges." In *Crossing Boundaries: Feminisms and the Critique of Knowledge,* edited by B. Caine, E. Grosz and M. de Lepervance. Sydney: Allen and Unwin, 1988.

Grosz, E. *Sexual Subversions: Three French Feminists.* Sydney: Allen and Unwin, 1989.

Grosz, E. "Contemporary Theories of Power and Subjectivity." In *Feminist Knowledge: Critique and Construct,* edited by Sneja Gunew. London & NY: Routledge, 1990.

Habermas, J. *The Theory of Communicating Action.* Volume 1, *Reason and the Rationalization of Society.* Boston: Beacon Press, 1984.

Habermas, J. *The Philosophical Discourse of Modernity: Twelve Lectures.* Cambridge: MIT Press, 1987.

Haggis, J. "Gendering Colonialism or Colonizing Gender? Recent Women's Studies Approaches to White Women and the History of British Colonialism." *Women's Studies International Forum* 13(1/2): 105–115 (1990).

Haggis, J. *Gendering Colonialism and Feminist Historiography.* University of Waikato Women's Studies Occasional Paper Series, No 6. Waikato, New Zealand, 1992.

Handler, J. *The Conditions of Discretion: Autonomy, Community, Bureaucracy.* New York: Sage, 1986.

Handler, J. "Dependent People, the State and the Modern/Postmodern Search for the Dialogic Community." *UCLA Law Review* 35: 999–1113 (1988).

Haraway, D. "Reading Buchi Emecheta: Contests for Women's Experience in Women's Studies." *Inscriptions* 3/4: 107–127 (1988).

Haraway, D. "A Manifesto for Cyborgs: Science, Technology and Socialist Feminism in the 1980's." In *Feminism/Postmodernism,* edited by L. Nicholson. New York and London: Routledge, 1990.

Hindess, B. "Citizenship in the Modern West." In *Citizenship,* edited by B.S. Turner. London: Sage, 1992.

Hobbes, T. *Leviathan* (Macpherson edition). Harmondsworth, Middlesex: Penguin Books, 1968.

Hobsbawm, E., and T. Ranger, eds. *The Invention of Tradition.* Cambridge: Cambridge University Press, 1983.

Hoffe, O. "Social Rights as Opposed to the Minimal State: A Philosophical 'Explanation'." *Labor and Society* 8(2): 179–195 (1983).

hooks, b. *Feminist Theory: From Margin to Center.* Boston: South End Press, 1984.

Jagose, A. "Slash and Suture: Post/Colonialism in *Borderlands*/La Frontera: *The New Mestiza.*" In *Feminism and the Politics of Difference,* edited by Sneja Gunew and Anna Yeatman. Sydney: Allen & Unwin, 1993.

John, M. "Postcolonial Feminists in the Western Intellectual Field: Anthropologists *and* Native Informants?" *Inscriptions* 5: 49–75 (1989).

Jolly, M. "Colonizing Women and Material Empire." In *Feminism and the Politics of Difference,* edited by Sneja Gunew and Anna Yeatman. Sydney: Allen & Unwin, 1993.

Klein, H. "Marxism, Psychoanalysis and Mother Nature." *Feminist Studies,* 15: 255–279 (1989).

Konrad, G., and I. Szelenyi. *The Intellectuals on the Road to Class Power.* New York and London: Harcourt, Brace, Jovanovich, 1979.

Kress, G. *Linguistic Processes in Sociocultural Practice.* Victoria: Deakin University Press, 1985.

Kukathas, C. "Are There Any Cultural Rights?" *Political Theory* 20 (1): 105–139 (1992).

Landes, J. *Women and the Public Sphere in the Age of the French Revolution.* Ithaca and London: Cornell University Press, 1988.

Lasch, C. *Haven in a Heartless World: The Family Besieged.* New York: Basic Books, 1977.

Leach, W. *True Love and Perfect Union: The Feminist Reform of Sex and Society.* New York: Basic Books, 1980.

Lemert, C. "Future of the Sixties Generation and Social Theory." *Theory and Society* 17: 789–807 (1988).

Levine, D. "Political Economy and the Argument for Inequality." *Social Concept* 2(3): 3–71 (1985).

Locke, J. *Two Treatises of Government* (Laslett edition). N.Y.: Cambridge University Press/Mentor, 1965.

Lyotard, J. F. *Heidegger and the "jews."* Minneapolis: University of Minnesota Press, 1990.

Lyotard, J. F. *The Postmodern Condition.* Manchester: Manchester University Press, 1984.

McHugh, P. *The Māori Magna Carta: New Zealand Law and the Treaty of Waitangi.* Auckland: Oxford University Press, 1991.

Macpherson, C. B. *The Political Theory of Possessive Individualism: Hobbes to Locke.* Oxford: Oxford University Press, 1962.

Mani, L. "Multiple Mediations: Feminist Scholarship in the Age of Multinational Reception." *Inscriptions* 5: 1–25 (1989).

Marcus, J. "Introduction: Anthropology, Culture and Post-Modernity." In *Writing Australian Culture: Text, Society and National Identity,* edited by J. Marcus. *Social Analysis* 27: 3–16, (1990).

Marshall, T. H. *Class, Citizenship and Social Development.* Chicago: University of Chicago Press, 1977.

Martin, B., and C. Mohanty. "Feminist Politics: What's Home Got to Do With It?" In *Feminist Studies/Critical Studies,* edited by T. de Lauretis. Bloomington: Indiana University Press, 1986 .

Marx, K. *Capital: Volume One.* Moscow: Progress Publishers, 1965.

Melucci, A. "Social Movements and the Democratization of Everyday Life." In *Civil Society and the State,* edited by I. Keane. London: Verso, 1988.

Melucci, A. *Nomads of the Present.* London: Hutchinson, 1989.

Miller, A. *The Drama of the Gifted Child.* New York: Basic Books, 1981.

Miller, A. *For Your Own Good: Hidden Cruelty in Child-Rearing and the Roots of Violence.* New York: Farrer, Strauss, Giroux, 1983.

Miller, A. *Thou Shalt Not Be Aware: Society's Betrayal of the Child.* New York: Farrar, Strauss, Giroux, 1984.

Miller, J. "Imperial Seductions." In *Seductions: Studies in Reading and Culture* London: Virago, 1990.

Mohanty, C. "Under Western Eyes: Feminist Scholarship and Colonial Discourses." *Feminist Review* 30: 61–89, (1988).

Mohanty, S.P. "Us and Them: On the Philosophical Bases of Political Criticism." *Yale Journal of Criticism* 2: (2): 1–32 (1989).

Nicholson, L. "Introduction." In *Feminism/Postmodernism,* edited by L. Nicholson. New York and London: Routledge, 1990.

Nietzsche, F. *Daybreak.* Cambridge: Cambridge University Press, 1982.

Ong, A. "Colonialism and Modernity: Feminist Re-Presentations of Women in Non-Western Societies." *Inscriptions* 3/4: 79–94, (1988).

Parsons, T. *Social Structure and Personality.* New York: Free Press, 1964.

Parsons, T. *The Structure of Social Action.* New York: Free Press, 1968.

Pateman, C."The Patriarchal Welfare State" In *The Disorder of Women.* Cambridge: Polity Press, 1987.

Pateman, C. *The Sexual Contract.* Cambridge: Polity Press, 1988.

Pisier, E. "The State in Current French Thought: End of an Era." *Thesis Eleven* 26: 95–110 (1990).

Rancière, J. "Politics, Indentification, and Subjectivization." *October* 61:12–20 (1992).

Rawls, J. *A Theory of Justice.* Oxford: Oxford University Press, 1971.

Riley, D. *"Am I that Name?" Feminism and the Category of "Women" in History.* London: Macmillan, 1988.

Rorty, R. *Philosophy and the Mirror of Nature.* Oxford: Basil Blackwell, 1979.

Rousseau, J. *The Social Contract and Discourses.* Translated by G.D.H. Cole. London: Dent, 1968.

Ryan, M. *Politics and Culture: Working Hypotheses for a Post-Revolutionary Society.* London: Macmillan, (1989).

Ryan, M. "Postmodern Politics." *Theory, Culture and Society* 5: 559–576 (1988).

Said, E. "Representing the Colonized: Anthropology's Interlocutors." *Critical Inquiry* 15: 205–226 1989.

Sawer, M. *Sisters in Suits: Women and Public Policy in Australia.* Sydney: Allen & Unwin, 1990.

Schrift, A. "The Becoming Post-Modern of Philosophy," In *After the Future: Postmodern Times and Places,* edited by G. Shapiro. Albany: SUNY Press, 1990.

Shapiro, M. *The Politics of Representation.* Madison: University of Wisconsin Press, 1988.

Sharp, A. "Representing *Justice and the Maori*: On Why It Ought Not to Be Considered a Postmodernist Text." *Political Theory Newsletter* 4: 27–38 (1992).

Sharp, A. *Justice and the Maori.* Auckland: Oxford University Press, 1990.

Smith, R. "Order and Disorder: The Naturalization of Poverty." *Cultural Critique* 14: 209–130 (1989–1990).

Smith, A. *The Wealth of Nations* (Canaan edition). Modern Library, 1937.

Smith, B. "Between a Rock and a Hard Place: Relationships between Black and Jewish Women." In E. Bulkin, M. Pratt and B. Smith. *Yours in Struggle: Three Feminist Perspectives on Anti-Semitism and Racism.* Ithaca, N.Y.: Long Haul Press, 1984.

Spivak, G. "Feminism and Deconstruction, Again: Negotiating with Unacknowledged Masculinism." In *Between Feminism and Psychoanalysis,* edited by T. Brennan. London and New York: Routledge, 1989.

Spoonley, P. "Pakeha Ethnicity: A Response to Māori Sovereignty." In P. Spoonley et al., eds. *Nga Take: Ethnic Relations and Racism in Aotearoa/New Zealand.* Palmerston North: Dunmore Press, 1992.

Stasiulius, D. "Theorizing Connections: Gender, Race, Ethnicity and Class." In *Race and Ethnic Relations in Canada,* edited by Peter Li. Toronto: Oxford University Press, 1990.

Stephanson, A. "Interview with Cornel West." In *Universal Abandon: The Politics of Postmodernism,* edited by A. Ross. Minneapolis: University of Minnesota Press, 1988.

Strathern, M. *The Gender of the Gift.* Berkeley and Los Angeles: University of California Press, 1988.

Szelenyi, I., and B. Martin. "The Three Waves of New Class Theories." *Theory and Society* 17: 645–667 (1988).

Threadgold, T. "Semiotics-Ideology-Language." In *Language, Semiotics, Ideology,* edited by T. Threadgold et al. Sydney Studies in Society and Culture no. 3. Sydney: Pathfinder Press, 1986.

Todorov, T. *Mikhail Bakhtin: The Dialogical Principle.* Minneapolis: University of Minnesota Press, 1984.

Trinh Minh-ha, T. "Of Other Peoples: Beyond the Salvage Paradigm." In *Dia Art Foundation Discussions in Contemporary Culture Number One,* edited by H. Foster. Seattle: Bay Press, 1987.

Trinh Minh-ha, T. "Not You/Like You: Colonial Women and the Interlocking Questions of Identity and Difference." *Inscriptions* 3/4: 71–79 (1988).

Tuck, R. *Natural Rights Theories: Their Origin and Development.* Cambridge: Cambridge University Press, 1979.

Turner, B.S. "Research Note: From Orientalism to Global Sociology." *Sociology* 23: 629–638 (1989).

Turner, B.S. "Periodization and Politics in the Postmodern." In *Theories of Modernity and Postmodernity,* edited by B.S. Turner. London: Sage, 1990.

Van Reijen, W., and D. Veerman. "An Interview with Jean-François Lyotard." *Theory, Culture and Society* 5: 277–309 (1988).

Wallace, M. "Reading 1968 and the Great American Whitewash." In *Remaking History.* Dia Art Foundation Discussions in Contemporary Culture Number One, edited by B. Kruger and P. Mariani. Seattle: Bay Press, 1989.

Wallis, B., ed. *Hans Haacke: Unfinished Business.* New York and Cambridge: The New Museum of Contemporary Art and MIT Press, 1986.

136 / Consolidated Bibliography

Walzer, M. _Spheres of Justice: A Defense of Pluralism and Equality._ Oxford: Basil Blackwell, 1983.

Waring, M. _Counting for Nothing: What Men Value and Women are Worth._ Wellington: New Zealand: Allen and Unwin/Port Nicholson Press, 1988.

Weber, M. _Economy and Society, Volume One._ Edited by G. Roth and C. Wittich. N.Y: Bedminster Press, 1968.

Weber, M. "Politics as a Vocation," In _From Max Weber,_ edited by H. H. Gerth and C. W. Mills. London: Routledge and Kegan Paul, 1970.

Weber, M. "'Objectivity' in Social Science and Social Policy." In M. Weber, _The Methodology of the Social Sciences,_ edited by E. Shils and H. Finch. New York: Free Press, 1989.

West, C. "Black Culture and Postmodernism." In _Remaking History,_ Dia Art Foundations Discussion in Contemporary Culture Number 4, edited by B. Kruger and P. Mariani. Seattle: Bay Press: 87–97, 1989.

Winnicott, D. W. _The Maturational Processes and the Facilitating Environment: Studies in the Theory of Emotional Development._ London: Hogarth Press, 1965.

Wolin, S. _Politics and Vision: Continuity and Innovation in Western Political Thought._ London: Allen and Unwin, 1961.

Yeatman, A. "The Classical Theory of Civil Society: An Analytic Critique." Ph.D. diss. State University of New York at Binghampton, 1980.

Yeatman, A. "Despotism and Civil Society: The Limits of Patriarchal Citizenship." In _Women's Views of the Political World of Men,_ edited by J. H. Stiehm. Dobbs Ferry, New York: Transnational Publishers, 1984.

Yeatman, A. "A Feminist Theory of Social Differentiation." In _Feminism/Postmodernism,_ edited by L. Nicholson. New York: Routledge, 1990(a).

Yeatman, A. _Bureaucrats, Technocrats, Femocrats: Essays on the Contemporary Australian State._ Sydney: Allen & Unwin, 1990(b).

Yeatman, A. "Voice & Representation in the Politics of Difference." In _Feminism and The Politics of Difference,_ edited by S. Gunew and A. Yeatman. Sydney: Allen & Unwin, 1993.

Young, I. "The Ideal of Community and The Politics of Difference." In _Feminism/Postmodernism,_ edited by L. Nicholson. NY & London: Routledge, 1990(a).

Young, I. _Justice and the Politics of Difference._ Princeton: Princeton University Press, 1990(b).

Young, I. "Together in Difference: Transforming the Logic of Group Political Conflict." _Political Theory Newsletter_ 4: 11–127 (1992).

Yuval-Davis, N. "The Citizenship Debate: Women, Ethnic Processes and the State." _Feminist Review_ 39: 54–69 (1991).

Index

Aboriginals, viii, xi, 5, 77, 93, 103, 128
Accountability, 22–24, 35, 36, 37, 45, 50,
    51–53; intellectual, xi, 22; political, xi,
    52–53, 96, 120
Action, corporative idea, 68–71; modern idea,
    58–66, 67–68, 69–70, 71
Advocacy, 36, 52, 99, 108; self-advocacy, 6
Agency, 5, 59
Anomie, 1, 10, 25
Anthropology, 21, 32, 48
Antimodernism, vii
Anzaldua, Gloria, 28
Assimilation(ism), 5, 29, 30, 86, 100; post-
    assimilationist, 86
Audiences, xi, 15, 22–24, 34, 36, 37
Australia, xi–xii, 5, 80, 86, 93, 94, 96, 101,
    102–103; South, xi, 50, 102, 128
Australian Government, 39, 50, 86, 102, 107,
    108
Australians, viii, 93, 95, 117, 128
Australian higher education, 38, 45, 102, 103
Authority, vii, viii, x, 31, 37, 43, 50, 59, 60, 61,
    63, 64, 67; crisis, 27, 31; intellectual, 15,
    22–24, 29, 32, 33, 37, 38, 42–43; profes-
    sional, xi, 27, 37, 38, 43, 68; of tradition,
    1, 59–60; sovereign, x; the public, 63–64,
    65, 66, 84

Bicultural(ism), xi, 44, 88, 93, 96
Binary(ies), 15, 16, 17, 18, 19, 24, 46, 47, 48,
    49, 127

Capitalism(t), 7, 9, 45; self-seeking, 66, 78
Cartesian philosophy, 2
Children, 62, 64, 65, 67–68, 71, 74, 75, 76, 77,

81, 82, 84, 85, 90, 94, 97, 98, 100
Chodorow, Nancy, 6, 78
Civil society, 69, 70, 76, 79
Civic culture, 44, 90, 91
Citizen (or, political) community, x, 4, 57–58,
    80, 82, 83, 84, 111
Citizenship, 57–58, 71, 73, 75, 76, 77, 80–81,
    82, 83, 86, 87, 91, 114; and difference,
    87–91; corporative, 57; liberal, 84, 85,
    108–109; modern, viii–ix, 84, 113; republi-
    can, 84–85, 108–109; social, 4–5, 72–75,
    86, 111, 112, 121; universal, 57, 75, 77–79;
    welfare-state, 76, 85, 90
Class, 18, 28, 31, 46, 47, 48, 53, 57, 87
Colonial(s), 29, 32, 33, 47; anti-colonial, 28;
    governmentality, 32. *See also* Postcolonial.
Colonialism, 4, 9, 97, 121
Colonies, 33
Colonization, xi, 9, 32, 44, 47–48; colonized,
    32, 44; colonized subjectivities, 28
Communicative action, 2, 84
Communism, 83
Community, 45, 58, 50, 52, 60, 63, 64, 65, 80,
    87, 92–105, 110, 111
Concepts, "analytic," 21; contestable, 25;
    generic, 20–21; genetic, 20–21; "indige-
    nous," 21
Connolly, William, 25
Contract, 65, 76, 82, 85
Critical theory, 43, 49–50; modern, 8; postmod-
    ern, vii, 2–3, 10
Cult of domesticity, 50, 71
Cultural exclusivism, 93, 95, 100, 104, 105
Cultural flexibility, 96
Cultural rights, 81, 82

Culture of rational enquiry, 43–46

Deconstruction(ive), 25, 42, 47, 49, 90, 100; relationship to modernity, vii, x, 2, 15, 16–17
De Lauretis, Teresa, 30, 49, 119, 123, 126
Democracy, 111; formal, 89; fratriarchal, 98; liberal, 90, 108, 115; modern, ix; plebiscitary, 43; postmodern, 115–116; social, 90, 113
Democratic, x. xi, 1, 2, 4, 9, 48, 50, 53, 74, 75, 77, 88, 89, 91, 96, 101, 102, 110, 111, 113, 125; different models, 6, 50, 52, 108; polity, x, 108, 109; socialism, 68; struggles, 4, 111, 113; theory, x; values, 102, 105, 122; vision, x
Derrida, Jacques, 5
Dialogic(al), 3, 14, 23, 32, 36, 40, 48, 51, 53, 84–85, 86, 87, 88, 89, 91; rights, 90
Dialogue, ix, 37, 43, 50, 52, 75, 89, 93, 113
Difference, vii, 5–6, 7, 16, 18, 24, 28, 40, 81, 83, 87, 107, 113, 115, 118; gender, 14; politics of, xi, 14–15, 19, 30, 32, 41, 48, 50, 53, 80, 89, 90, 91, 95, 110, 119–120, 125, 129
Differentiation, 18, 40, 50, 71, 87
Discourse, 14, 21, 25, 37, 49
Discursive, 7, 13, 14, 15, 21, 23, 119, 120; discursive closure, 23, 25; discursive economy, 7; discursive formation, 14–15, 19, 30; discursive innocence, 7; discursive management, 31; discursive order, 7, 14; discursive regime, 7; discursive space, 14, 23; discursive struggles, 23; discursive tradition, 9
Division of labor in society, 57, 68, 70–71, 73, 84
Domestic despotism, 62, 64, 71, 82
Donzelot, Jacques, 76, 109
Durkheim, Emile, 57, 68–70, 74–75, 109, 127

Economy, 91, 109, 111; discursive, 7; of inclusions and exclusions, ix
Emancipation, 5–7, 60
Emancipatory, movements, vii, 5–6, 53; politics, vii–x, 5–6, 10, 118; project, 16; rhetoric, 5
Embodiment, 15, 19, 24, 85; embodied subject, 15, 24–25
Enlightenment, 2, 8
Environmentalist(m), 8, 121
Epistemology, 15–20, 28–29, 30, 32, 33, 42;

epistemological order, 31; epistemological politics, xi, 1, 13, 15, 31, 40, 43; epistemological spaces, 31
Equality, iii, ix, 47, 57, 61, 66, 126
Ethnic, 5, 29, 31, 46, 47, 48, 53, 87, 95, 96, 102
Ethnicity, 14, 18, 48, 87
Ethnocentric, 6
Expert (non-expert), 50–53

Family, 62, 66–67, 69, 71, 74, 79, 109
Feminism, 17, 43, 49, 53, 57, 83, 93, 99, 102, 118, 119, 123, 125; as critique, 47–50, 84, 85, 99–100; contemporary politics, 46–50; first wave, 45, 57; liberal, 13; postmodern, x, 15–26; radical, 13, 48; relationship to postmodernism, 13, 24, 25, 28; second wave, 45; socialist, 13; western, 13, 34, 46, 47; white settler, xii; women's movements of Australia and New Zealand, xii, 102
Feminist, 30–31, 33, 35, 104, 125; community, 50; intellectuals, 30–32, 39, 42; postcolonial, 13, 28; specification of agency, 6; theory(izing), 13, 15–26, 28, 48–50, 78, 124
Femocracy, 47
Foucauldian, 3, 30
Foucault, Michel, viii, 116
Foundation(alist), 13, 28–30, 33, 35, 36, 37, 40, 41, 82; post-foundationalist, 30, 32, 35–36, 37, 39, 41
Freedom, 59–61, 64–65, 85
Freud, Sigmund, 78

Gatens, Moira, 16, 17, 24
Gender, 14, 16, 17, 18, 25, 31, 43, 46, 47, 48, 87, 93, 120; division of labor, 47
Global, 31, 80
Globalized, 4, 27, 80
Governance, ix, 3, 81, 96, 109, 111, 113; academic-collegial, 43
Government, 29, 43–44, 50, 52, 61, 62–63, 64, 71; democratic, 60, 62; domestic, 62, 67, 71, 77; patrimonial, 60–61, 67; self-, 60
Governmentality, 32
Grosz, Liz, 15, 19–20, 24

Habermas, Jürgen, viii, 2, 20, 31, 84–85
Handler, Joel, 87, 88, 90
Hegel, G.W.F., vßiii, x
Hindess, Barry, 80, 85
Hobbes, Thomas, 59, 65, 102, 126
hooks, bell, 35, 46–47

Humanities, 42, 48

Identity, 23, 30, 80, 81, 83, 88, 90, 114, 118–119, 120–121; games, 18; hybridized (hyphenated) identities, 19, 96;politics, xi, 16, 23, 83
Imbrication, 14, 20
Immigration law and policy, 95, 111, 118
Individual, 90, 92, 107, 119, 128; freedom, 57–61, 64–65, 69, 72, 76, 77; individual/society, 60, 78; liberal (see also Natural right), 81–82, 84; rights, 72–73 74, 75, 81; self-determination, x, 58, 60, 78
Individualism, x, 79, 82; possessive, 70
Individuality, 58, 60–61, 64, 69, 74, 78, 84, 85, 90, 91; relational, 6
Intellectuals, 28, 33, 53; feminist, 30–31, 33, 35, 39, 42, 52–53; oppositional, 28–31, 37; postcolonial, 30–31, 33; subaltern, xi, 30, 32–34

Justice, x, 1, 2, 42, 43, 86, 87, 88, 93, 95, 106, 117, 120, 124, 125

Knowledge, applied, 38; claims, 1, 13, 32, 37, 45, 48, 50; expert, 51, 52; production, 42; professional(ized), xi, 38–40; situated, 9, 19
Kukathas, Chandran, 81–82

Labor (Party of Australia), 102, 104
Landes, Joan, 24, 84, 126
Language politics, 15, 25, 113–117
Levine, David, 78
Liberalism, 81–82, 83, 84, 85, 90, 91, 108
Locke, John, x, 21, 59–60, 61–65, 67, 69, 81, 102, 103, 126, 127
Lyotard, J.-F., x, 1, 82, 85, 106, 110, 111, 113, 116, 117, 121, 129

Macpherson, C.B., 70
Managerialism, 43, 110
Maori, xi, 3, 43, 52, 87–88, 93, 96, 117, 120–121, 127
Marae, 3
Market, 9, 41, 66, 77, 83, 84, 85, 91, 92, 111
Marshall, T.H., 72–73, 76, 85, 127
Marx, x, 25, 69, 70
Marxism(t), 25, 33, 103
Melucci, Alberto, 108, 113, 114–116, 129
Miller, Alice, 78–79
Minorities, 84–85, 86

Modern, citizenship, viii, 84–86; critical theory, 8; democratic politics, ix; emancipatory project, ix, 7–9; politics, x; rationalism, 9; values of rationalism and universalism, vii, viii, x
Modernity, 2, 7–9
Mohanty, S.P., 5–6
Montesquieu, 102, 126
Moral terror, 46
Multiculturalism, xi, 86, 89, 93, 95, 96, 99, 102, 104

Nation, 93
National community (see also citizen community), 92–105; conventionalist accounts, 94, 95–96, 100–103, 104, 105 customary accounts; 94–95, 96–100, 101, 103, 104–105
Nationalism, 4, 96–97, 100
National liberation, 4, 28
Nationhood, 4, 93
Natural right, 57–70, 103, 104, 109
Needs, expert-defined, 39–40, 51–52, 53, 107, 108; expressed, 39–40, 51–52, 53, 89, 107; politics of needs-formation, 106–108
Needs-based planning, 39–40, 86–87
Negotiated settlements, 2–3, 7, 51, 82, 86, 88, 89, 90, 107–108, 115–116, 120–121
Negotiation, 2, 3
Neo-Kantian, 2, 6
New World, 101–102, 104
New Zealand, xi-xii, 3, 21, 44, 45, 80, 88, 93, 94, 96, 101, 102, 103, 120, 127–128
Nietzsche(an), 30, 48, 97, 98, 124
Object relations theory, 78
Observer, 27, 37; problematic of, 32, 36, 37, 39

Pakeha, xi, 3, 87–88, 93, 96, 120, 121, 127–128
Parsons, Talcott, 20, 126, 127
Partnership model, 51–52, 88
Pateman, Carole, 77, 84, 98
Paternalistic protection, 98–100, 110
Performativity, x, 14, 110–117, 121
Perspectivalism, 1, 2, 15, 17, 19, 20, 24, 30, 34, 37, 87, 107
Philosophical anthropology, 5–6
Plato, 1
Policy, 52–53, 57, 73, 86, 89, 95, 97–99, 100–101, 102, 107, 109, 110, 111, 113, 115
Policy-makers, 38, 101
Polis, 97
Political community, ix, 58, 60, 64, 65, 66, 69,

70–71, 75, 76, 77, 79, 88–89, 90
Politics, epistemological, xi, 1, 13, 15, 31, 40; of difference, xi, 14–15, 19, 30, 32, 41, 48, 50, 53, 80, 88, 89, 90, 91, 95, 110, 119–120, 121–122, 125, 129; of identity, xi; of location, 20; non-totalizing, 50; of voice and representation, x, xi, 2, 6, 9, 13, 48, 80, 81, 82, 110, 117; universally oriented, ix
Polity, x, 36, 38, 39–40, 55, 73, 83, 84, 86, 88, 89, 90, 95, 108, 109, 122
Popper, Karl, 31
Positioning (positionality), xi, 5, 7, 14, 15, 17, 19, 20, 22–24, 30, 31, 37, 89, 119, 125
Positivism, 3–4
Postcapitalist, 7
Postcolonial(ism), vii, xi–xii, 9, 14, 20, 27, 33, 57, 93, 96, 104, 122, 128; anthropologies, 21; discourses, 14; feminist theorists, 13, 28, 34; movements, 4, 5, 28, 99–100; politics, 4; theorists, 27, 32–33
Postdisciplinary, 1
Postmodern, 1; critical theory, vii, 3, 5, 9; emancipatory politics, ix–x, 6–7; emancipatory vision, ix; moment, vii, ix; political project, vii; politics, ix, x, 121–122
Postmodernism, vii–xii, 2, 9, 13, 27, 123
Postmodernity, 7–9, 106, 112–113
Post-universalistic, 15, 17
Pragmatics, 1, 2, 5, 6, 8, 23, 98, 102; of knowledge, 20, 23; pragmatically oriented settlements, 22, 82, 106, 120
Pratt, Minnie Bruce, 50, 119, 126
Private property (modern idea), 61–63, 64–66, 67–68, 91, 98, 102, 103–104
Proceduralism, 3, 29, 89
Professional(s), 27, 19, 36, 39, 50, 52, 70, 106, 108, 109, 116, 128; authority, xi, 27, 37; domination, 38, 39, 50, 51, 52, 107; expertise, xi, 27, 50;-client relationship, 36; service-deliverers, 38, 77, 116–117
Professionalism, 45, 50, 125
Professionalization, 45
Professionalized knowledge, xi
Progress, 8
Progressives(ism), 57, 85
Public, the, 80–81
Public goods and values, 92–93, 94
Public intellectual, 53
Public learning, 101
Publics, 20–22
Public spaces, ix, 31, 108, 111–113, 114, 115

Race, 14, 17, 18, 31, 46, 47, 48, 53, 57, 87, 115, 117
Racism (anti-), 27, 46, 117–118, 126, 129
Rational action, 6, 40
Rational choice, 6
Rational inquiry, 43, 45, 46
Rationalism(t), vii, viii, x, 9, 29; monocultural, 29, 35, 43, 46, 85; utopianism, 6, 7
Rational legal order, 81
Rational metaphysics, 27
Rational patriarchs, 43, 44
Reason, idea of rational consensus, x, 2, 42, 84, 107, 122; transcendental, 1, 2, 9; univocal, x, 9, 29
Relational theory of knowledge, 15, 30
Relativism, 6, 9, 15, 20, 30
Representation, x, 4, 6, 13, 14, 30; feminist, 49; politics of, x, 14, 31, 35, 37–38, 48, 49, 111, 114, 119; -al praxis, x
Revolution (idea of), 7, 8
Rhetoric, 4–5, 49, 53, 107, 111, 112, 121, 122, 128
Rhetorical practice/praxis, 23, 111, 113, 114, 121
Rhetorical procedures, 119
Rousseau, J.-J., x, 59, 61, 63, 69, 85, 103, 126

Said, Edward, 27, 28, 32, 39, 125
Saussure(an), 13, 14
Science, 8, 29, 31, 33, 35, 42, 51; post-foundationalist, 35
Scientific objectivity, 29, 45
Scientistic(ism), 25, 46
Scientists, 28; subaltern, 29–30
Search technique, 89
Self(ves), 5, 18, 78–79, 82–83, 89, 90, 119; -government, 60–61, 119; /other relationship, 83, 90
Self-determination, x, xi, 5–6, 7, 58, 60, 64, 65, 66, 69, 70, 71, 73, 74, 75, 79, 80, 84, 85, 91, 100, 108, 117
Self-presence, 18
Self-representation, 6
Service delivery, 50–52, 86, 88, 100, 101, 113, 114; democratic, 52, 107; partnership, 51–51, 88
Sexuality, 14, 48, 87, 114
Sharp, Andrew, 87–88, 100, 120–121
Skepticism, 48
Smith, Barbara, 117–118, 129
Social contract, 63, 81, 102, 103, 127

Social movements, 5, 28, 37, 45, 107, 110, 111, 113–116, 117, 118–120, 123, 126, 129
Social science, 1, 17, 19, 20, 21, 25, 26, 27, 48
Social system, 70, 110, 112, 115
Social theory, 1, 20, 25
Social welfare, 111
Sociology of knowledge (producers), 33, 46
Sovereign(ty), x, 94, 120, 128
Standards of validity, 2–3
State, 9, 38, 57, 66, 67–68, 69, 71–77, 79, 81, 84, 89, 92–105, 109, 110–113, 115, 117, 120, 121 (see also welfare-state); competition, 111–112; interventionist, 66, 72, 76, 101, 103, 105, 109–110; liberal/republican, 112; minimal, 58, 66, 72, 76; sovereign, x, 94
Strategies of public address, 22
Subaltern, constituencies, 33, 35, 36; intellectuals, xi, 33–35; scientists, 29–30
Subject, 14, 20; discursively interpellated, 14–15, 19; humanist, 5; individualized, 3; of politics, x; subject/object epistemological relationship, 29–30, 32, 33, 36, 40; tribal, 3; unitary, 13; universal/historical, viii, 5–6, 16, 118; universal/impartial sovereign subject, x, 2, 17, 29

Technical, 8
Technological, 4, 8; high-tech, 4, 25; technology(ies), 14, 19
Terror, 46, 83, 111, 112, 113, 115, 117, 119
Third World, 4, 118, 129; leadership, 4
Tradition, vii, 1, 60, 90, 97, 120; (al) time, 8
Treaty of Waitangi, 87–88, 121
Turner, B.S., viii, 125

Tutelage, 76–77, 79, 85
Universal, 24; knower, 42; reason, 29; standards of validity, 2
Universalism, vii, viii, x; monocentric, 13; monorational, 43, 81
Universalistic, ix, 15
University, xi, 42–46, 52–53; Academy, 34, 45, 36, 37, 38; autonomy, 43, 45; democratization of, 37, 45; idea of, 43, 44; of Waikato, xi, xii, 44; western, 31
Utopian(n)(dystopian), 6–7, 16, 82

Value neutrality, 45
Values, 30, 37, 42, 44, 45, 48, 52, 101, 126

Weber, Max, 6, 20, 64, 81, 89, 98
Welfare-state, 4, 57, 71, 72, 75, 76–77, 78, 79, 84, 85, 86, 94, 104, 107, 109, 111, 112, 121, 129; politics, 5
West, 121, 129
Western, 1, 4, 5, 9, 16, 21, 22, 32, 40, 118, 122; epistemology, 40, 42; feminism, 13; ideals and values, 44, 45; imperialism, 4, 9, 14, 32, 47–48; university, 31
Women, viii, 16, 17, 24, 27, 30, 33, 42, 43, 44, 46–48, 49, 52, 57, 64, 67, 71, 75, 85, 90, 93, 94, 95, 98, 100, 114, 117, 119, 123, 125; Black, 117–118; of colour, 46; Jewish, 117–118; movements, xi, 42–48, 52–53
Women's Studies, xi, 42–48, 52–53
Working class, 4

Yeats, W. B., 1
Young, Iris, 48, 83, 84, 87, 125